LANGUAGE LESSONS

Leaving Certificate English Paper 1 (Ordinary Level)

Dan Stynes

g GILL EDUCATION

Gill Education
Hume Avenue
Park West
Dublin 12
www.gilleducation.ie

Gill Education is an imprint of M.H. Gill & Co.

ISBN: 978-0-7171-88093

Design: Westchester Publishing Services
Print origination: Carole Lynch

At the time of going to press, all web addresses were active and contained information relevant to the topics in this book. Gill Education does not, however, accept responsibility for the content or views contained on these websites. Content, views and addresses may change beyond the publisher or author's control. Students should always be supervised when reviewing websites.

For permission to reproduce text, the authors and publisher gratefully acknowledge the following:
'Why Black Lives Matter', speech given by Alicia Garza at the Citizen University Annual National Conference in the United States. Published 18 March 2016 by Citizen University on opentranscripts.org. © 2016 Alicia Garza.
'Working 12-hour days and moving 400,0000 tonnes of snow', news report by Paul Hosford, published 6 March 2018 by TheJournal.ie. Edited and reproduced with the permission of TheJournal.ie.
'Gen Z kids are the stars of their parents' social media - and they have opinions about that' article by Caitlin Gibson, published 3 June 2019 by The Washington Post. © 2019 The Washington Post. All rights reserved. Used under license.
Extract from *Can You See Me* by Libby Scott and Rebecca Westcott. Text © Rebecca Westcott, 2019. Diary Entries © Libby Scott, 2019. Reproduced with the permission of Scholastic Limited. All rights reserved.
Extract from *Oh My God, What A Complete Aisling* by Emer McLysaght and Sarah Breen. © 2017 Emer McLysaght and Sarah Breen. Reproduced by permission of Gill Books.
'The Nine Mental Skills of Successful Athletes' article, copyright © 1998 Ohio Center for Sport Psychology. Reproduced by kind permission of the author, Jack J. Lesyk.
Extract from *Recovering* by Richie Sadlier. © 2019 Richie Sadlier. Reproduced by permission of Gill Books.
The Secret Footballer's Guide to the Modern Game: Tips and Tactics from the Ultimate Insider by The Secret Footballer. Copyright © The Secret Footballer, 2014. Published by Guardian Faber.

For permission to reproduce photographs, the author and publisher gratefully acknowledge the following:
© Alamy: ixB, 5, 20T, 20B, 30L, 30R, 40, 55R, 67L, 67R, 77, 86, 105, 106, 121, 128, 131, 132, 144T, 146, 151, 160, 167; © Anders Hellberg: 84L; © AP/Shutterstock: 37B; © Cristiana Couceiro: 18; © DAA: 28; © Getty Images: 1, 4, 7, 13, 18, 39, 42, 46, 71, 74L, 76, 89, 91, 98, 103, 108, 116, 123, 125, 129, 137, 140, 143, 145, 152, 154, 159, 166, 170, 175, 181; © Gill Books: 65, 94R; © Inpho: 74R; © Johnny Silvercloud: 18; © The O'Brien Press: 136; © Penguin Random House: 57; © Photosport: 72; © Rawpixel: 50; © Reuters: 48; © RTÉ: ixT, 32, 84R; © Scholastic: 55L; © Shutterstock: 21, 52, 80, 99, 100, 110, 144B, 161, 176, 179, 187; © Sportsfile: 94L; © Thomas Taylor, used by permission of Bloomsbury Publishing Plc: 114; Courtesy of The Basket Room: 117; Courtesy of Foróige: 51; Courtesy of The Irish Men's Shed Association: 184; Courtesy of NornIronGirl1981/Bronagh McAtasney: 36–37; Courtesy of So Sue Me/Suzanne Jackson: 59; Courtesy of Women on Writing: 96.

The authors and publisher have made every effort to trace all copyright holders. If, however, any have been inadvertently overlooked, we would be pleased to make the necessary arrangement at the first opportunity.

The paper used in this book is made from the wood pulp of managed forests. For every tree felled, at least one tree is planted, thereby renewing natural resources.

CONTENTS

Composing

LEAVING CERTIFICATE PAPER 1

Introduction

The Leaving Certificate Paper 1 is divided into two sections: Comprehending (Section I: A – Reading Comprehension and B – Functional Writing) and Composing (Section II: Personal Essay, Short Story, Speech, and Article). You will need to answer one Reading Comprehension question, one Functional Writing question, and one Composition question.

Getting the points in the Leaving Certificate examination

Leaving Certificate English is marked using the **PCLM** marking scheme. **PCLM** stands for **purpose (P)**, **coherence (C)**, **language (L)**, **mechanics (M)**. It is important that you understand these terms and keep them in mind when you are writing your answers.

Purpose – 30% of marks

The first thing the examiner looks for is whether you have **answered the question**. You will be given a specific task such as 'Write an **article**', or 'Give **your impression** of the author of the text'. You must make sure you do *exactly* what you are asked and not wander off-topic.

You also have to make sure you answer **all parts** of the question. Some questions will have two or three parts, and each part must be answered or you will lose marks automatically.

Lastly, the examiner will decide on **how well** you have answered the question. This means that two students could use the same ideas, but whoever writes a better answer will get more **purpose** marks.

Coherence – 30% of marks

The next thing the examiner looks at is **how well your answer is structured**. Does it have an **introduction** where you set out your ideas? Do your **ideas** have **references** and examples? Do you **explain** your ideas fully? Are your paragraphs **linked**? Do you sum up your points in the **conclusion**?

Language – 30% of marks

Here the examiner is assessing **how well you have written** your answer. Is your **vocabulary** of a high standard? Have you **varied** your **sentence structure**? Have you used **descriptive terms**?

Mechanics – 10% of marks

Although it only counts for one tenth of your marks, **mechanics** impacts on the rest of your work. Marks are awarded for things like spelling, punctuation, grammar, and using the correct tense. If these things are not right, then your **purpose**, **coherence**, and **language** marks will all suffer.

How to structure an answer – Comprehending Question A

It is vital for your **coherence** mark that you pay close attention to the **structure** of your answers for both Comprehending Question A and Question B questions. Every answer you write should follow the same pattern:

- Introduction
- Main body
- Conclusion

1. Introduction

In this section you will:

- Give your opinion on the question
- Set out what you are going to speak about

In some questions you will need to include things that are necessary for that form of writing; for example, adding an address in a formal letter or a headline in a news report.

2. Main body

This is the main section of your answer. How long this section is depends on the number of marks available in the question, but, in each paragraph, you should:

- Write a full point using **IRE** (**Idea**, **Reference**, **Explain**)
- **Refer** back to the question at the end of the paragraph: 'This is a clear example of …' or '… which really shows how …'
- **Link** the paragraphs together using phrases like: 'Another point is …' or 'Secondly …' or 'Leading on from this …'

3. Conclusion

In this section you will:

- Sum up the points you have made
- Refer back to the question

In some questions you will need to do things that are necessary for a particular style or form of writing, such as signing your name in an **open letter**, or leaving the audience with a question in a **talk**.

Idea, Reference, Explain (IRE)

Every paragraph must have a **purpose**. If you follow the **IRE** approach, you will make a point in each paragraph you write. If you complete all the steps, every point will be of good quality and will be between 60 to 80 words, which is what you need for Ordinary Level.

I – IDEA

State your **idea** at the start of the paragraph. 'I think that the narrator in the text is …' Or 'From my reading of the piece, the main character comes across as …' Straight away, the reader knows exactly what your **idea** is and what point you are trying to make in the paragraph.

The **idea** is usually one sentence.

R – REFERENCE

Next you must show the reader (usually, your teacher, but in the Leaving Certificate it will be the examiner) where you got your information from by using a **direct quote** or **reference**.

A direct quote would be like this: **When the narrator says, 'I'll never forget the first time …'**

If you can't remember the quote or find the part in the text that you want to use, then you can **refer** to the text: **The narrator speaks about how they will never forget the first time …** Quotes are better than references, but make sure they are short (five to eight words long), as they are there to help you make the point, not *be* the point.

The **reference** is usually one sentence and can be added onto the end of the **idea** sentence.

E – EXPLAIN

This is the most important part of any paragraph. It is easy enough to come up with an **idea** and find a **reference** for it. The hardest part is **explaining** your point to the reader – giving your personal opinion on why or how the quote or reference you have chosen answers the question. This is where you can really stand out from others doing the same question.

Sample answer

Here is a sample answer to the Comprehending A Black Lives Matter question in Lesson 3 (pages 15–16). It uses the **IRE** approach to paragraphing. Watch for the **structure** and how the **key question** words are used. What do you think the strengths and weaknesses of this answer are?

> **I need three examples. Also, the question says 15 marks, so I'll need three main body paragraphs.**

> **I can only use the first four paragraphs in my answer.**

> **I'm looking for examples of racism in America.**

> **I am looking for the speaker's opinion, not my own.**

Based on your reading of the first four paragraphs, outline three examples of racism shown toward Black people in America given by the speaker. Support your answer with reference to the text. (15)

> **Introduction paragraph.**

> **Circle the parts of the first line that use the key question words.**

> **Number the three examples given in the introduction.**

Alicia Garza uses many examples of how racism has been, and still is, a part of American life, including: slavery, how Black people were treated differently to white people after Hurricane Katrina, and police killings.

(35 words)

> **The opening sentence contains both the idea and the reference. Mark both of them with an 'I' for idea and an 'R' for reference.**

> **Main body paragraph – racism example 1.**

> **A direct quote is used to back up the idea. That's why it is in speech marks.**

Firstly, she talks about slavery when she says how from 1619 'Black people were brought here in chains.' America had Black African slaves for hundreds of years and most of them were treated terribly by their owners. Many people in America today still have racist views of Black people because of their history of slavery and that is how slavery is still a part of American life.

(67 words)

A further example of racism is how Black people and white people were treated after Hurricane Katrina. Black people, according to Garza, were forced to go to huge stadiums in order to be safe. They were even shot at by police. White people, on the other hand, were praised for surviving. This shows racism, as white people were given better treatment even though everyone was going through the same thing.

(70 words)

> **Main body paragraph – racism example 2.**

> No **direct quote** is used. The writer only **refers** to the part in the text when Garza mentions Hurricane Katrina.

> **Main body paragraph – racism example 3.**

Finally, Garza talks about the police shooting of Tamir Rice, a kid who 'was shot and killed by police officers in Cleveland while playing alone in a park.' She mentions other people, such as Oscar Grant, who was also killed by police. She says that the police wouldn't treat white people like this, so this clearly shows that racism is still alive in America.

(64 words)

> The quote is 15 words long, nearly a quarter of the word count. Quotes should be a lot shorter, about 5 to 8 words.

> The **idea** and **quote** mention Tamir Rice, but the **explanation** refers to Oscar Grant. Why is this an example of bad writing?

> **Conclusion paragraph.**

> The **conclusion** clearly recaps the points made and refers back to the question.

Overall, by looking at slavery, the story of Hurricane Katrina, and police killings of Black people, Garza shows how racism is a part of American life, both in the past and now.

(32 words)

> Never use a writer's first name. Your answer should have a **formal tone**, so use their full name or just their surname.

How to structure an answer – Comprehending Question B

Before you answer a Question B, there are a number of things that you should keep in mind:

What exactly am I being asked?

This means you must look at the question *fully*. It's not enough to just glance at it. You need to see what type of functional writing question you are being asked for, and how many things you need to talk about in your answer.

What kind of writing is it?

Question B challenges you to write in a number of ways. Each form of writing will have a particular function or purpose. You could be asked to write a speech to inform or convince people. Or a letter to invite or nominate someone. Or a diary entry to show emotion and explain something. Figure out the function of your writing before you start.

Who is the audience?

Each question will be aimed at a particular audience. That audience will determine your register and tone, so it is really important to figure it out before you start. Is your speech for parents or First Years? Is your article aimed at young people or adults? Make sure you know before you start writing.

What register should I use?

Once you know your audience, you can figure out how you should to speak to them.

- A news report on RTÉ will be **formal**, meaning that you will have to be serious and not use any humour or slang. In many work situations, such as writing a letter of application, the tone needs to be formal.

RTÉ news reporter Caitríona Perry stands in front of her desk in the news room.

- A talk to staff at your school will be **semi-formal**. Yes, you will have to be serious, but you can bring in some light moments as well.

- A diary entry will be **informal**. You can write in a way that is totally free. You can use slang and use emotional language.

What tone should I use?

The **register** will have an effect on the **tone**. Your **tone** simply means the way you say the words. You can be serious when talking to a garda about bike safety. You can be sarcastic when attacking an opponent's point in a debate. You can be humorous when telling an anecdote in a talk. Make sure your tone suits the audience, the situation, and the topic you are writing or talking about.

What type(s) of language should I use?

In **Lesson 1** you will read about the different types of language: **information**, **argument**, **persuasion**, **narration**, and **aesthetic**. Your Question B answer will use a combination of these, depending on the function, task, and audience.

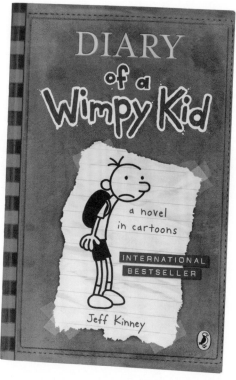

Diary of a Wimpy Kid by Jeff Kinney is one of the most famous fictional diaries in children's literature.

LANGUAGE SKILLS

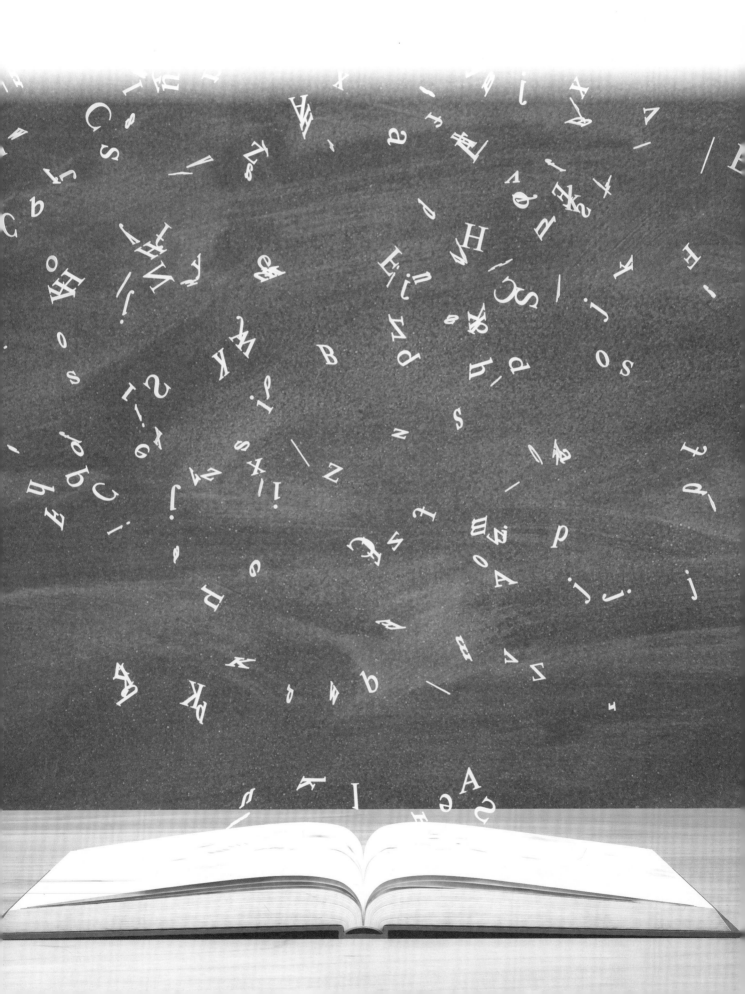

About this section: Language skills

Lessons 1–2 focus on general language skills, grammar and punctuation.

Exercises and sample answers aim to help you develop your written language skills across the whole paper.

LESSON 1: TYPES OF LANGUAGE

Learning Objectives – By the end of this lesson you should:

- Know the different types of language used in the Leaving Certificate
- Be able to identify examples of them
- Be able to write examples using each type of language

Types of language

There are many different ways to write. The Leaving Certificate challenges students to read, understand, and write in five different ways. These five ways of writing will continually mix and mingle within texts and genres.

1. **Language of information**

   The language of information is used when an idea is presented in a direct, objective, and factual way; for example, in a set of instructions or a news report.

2. **Language of persuasion**

   The language of persuasion is used when a writer wants to convince people of an argument or to persuade people to take their side. This is done using emotion – for example, sympathy, force, or cajoling – and is most often seen in speeches and talks.

3. **Language of argument**

   The language of argument uses facts and logic to make a point. Most of the time when you write in English class, you are arguing a point. You have been asked a question, then you give an answer. The best answers are always backed up with evidence, examples, and references.

4. **Language of narration**

   We are all very familiar with the language of narration or storytelling. When you talk to your friends about a night out you had, or a goal you scored, or any story you tell, you are narrating. We see this style of writing in novels, dramas, personal essays, and short stories.

5. **Aesthetic language**

   Aesthetic language is another word for descriptive language. It is used in famous works of literature to describe things in a poetic or beautiful way.

Question analysis

Look at the examples of writing about a library on the following pages:

- Identify the type of language
- Write one or two more sentences continuing the paragraph in the same type of language.

Ruth loved the library. It had been a part of her life ever since her mother brought her there to read the Mr Men and Little Miss books when she was a little girl. Now, as a teenager studying for exams, it remained a space close to her heart. She sat down in her usual spot and opened up her Maths book. Mr McCarthy was a scary man but one hell of a teacher. She needed to study hard or else he'd move her down. He was well known for being ruthless.

(92 words)

Type of language:_____

Continue the passage: _____

_____

_____

_____

There is just something about books. The sense of anticipation as you see the shelves. Your heart starts to race as you run your finger along the spines. The rough, leather-bound books tell you that this is a place not just for now, but for ever. My mind always thinks about the many who came before me, who turned each golden page as they became engrossed in places like Wonderland or Oz or Hogwarts.

(74 words)

Type of language:_____

Continue the passage: _____

_____

_____

_____

Look, I really need you to see where I'm coming from here. This library is _amazing_. It's been a part of our community for decades and does so much for us. You see happy kids playing and reading there. Reading! Not iPads, actual books! Think of all the good it is doing. Of how important it is to keep this facility open. You make the decisions with your feet. If you walk in and use it, you convince people to fund it. If you don't, they won't. I implore you; I beg you – use your library.

(96 words)

Type of language:_____

Continue the passage: _____

_____

_____

_____

A library houses a collection of books. One of the oldest public libraries opened in Dublin in 1707. It is called Archbishop Marsh's Library. Since then, countless public libraries have opened all over the world. Once you become a member of a library, you receive a library card. This entitles you to take out books and read them at home. Once you have finished with them, you return them for someone else to read. There used to be a fine for returning books late, but from 2019 these fines have been abolished.

(92 words)

Type of language:_____

Continue the passage: _____

_____

_____

_____

So why should we fund public libraries? I am here today to explain why. They are key centres of the community and not just places where you can take out books. There are children's playgroups, computers, printing facilities, meeting rooms, and even study groups. Others will say that they make no money, so keeping them open is a huge cost to the taxpayer. I say, that they make no money is a good thing. They are for the people, not for making profit.

(83 words)

Type of language:_____

Continue the passage: _____

_____

_____

_____

LESSON 2: GRAMMAR, SPELLING, AND PUNCTUATION REVISION

Learning Objectives – By the end of this lesson you should:

- Know why correct spelling, better punctuation, the correct use of capital letters, and using correct grammar is vital to writing a high-quality answer
- Be able to complete each exercise to a high standard
- Understand the importance of reading over your own work

 Time to Think

Do you read over your own writing when you are finished?

What about when your teacher hands you back your corrected work? Do you look over the comments and corrections? Many students don't. If you are one of them, why don't you?

It's very important that you start doing this. As stated in the Chief Examiner's Report for Leaving Certificate English in 2013, being able to 'draft, re-draft and edit' your own writing will only make it better. If you know where you are going wrong, then you will be able to improve it the next time.

PCLM

M – Spelling, grammar, punctuation, and capital letters are all important aspects of writing in English and are worth 10% of the marks in every question.

However, if your writing isn't up to standard, then it impacts your **purpose (P)**, **coherence (C)**, and **language (L)** marks as well, which combined are worth the remaining 90% of marks.

Exploring spelling

Read the following sentences and place the correct word in the blank space:

- There – place
- Their – belongs to them
- They're – short for 'they are'

1. 'I always wanted to go _____ but I could never get the time off,' Jack sighed.

2. 'The books? _____ on the floor beside the window,' Adam whispered. 'Beside _____ coats.'

3. The band played _____ instruments loudly into the night before heading over _____ to the hotel.

- Our – belongs to us
- Are – present tense (usually follows 'you,' 'we,' or 'they')

4. 'I am pretty good at football,' Mohammad said, 'but you _____ simply awesome.'

5. _____ club needed the funding to build a new clubhouse.

6. _____ drama group is performing tomorrow night in the Abbey and we _____ fantastic.

- Were – past tense of 'are' (usually follows 'you,' 'we,' or 'they')
- Where – a place. As a question, it's usually at the start of a sentence
- We're – short for 'we are'

7. '_____ on first, and then they're on after us,' Sandra explained.

8. We went to the field _____ the battle took place.

9. '_____ not going,' Nicole sighed, 'as the hotel _____ we were supposed to be staying has flooded.'

- Its – belonging to it
- It's – short for 'it is' or 'it has'

10. The turtle's head popped out of _____ shell.

11. '_____ the best I can do,' groaned Henry as he slumped to the ground.

12. The band said _____ been a long time since it played in _____ home town.

- Should've – short for 'should have'.
- Could've – short for 'could have'.

13. I _____ completed my homework, but I watched the match instead.

14. Mary _____ done the housework like her mother asked, but instead she went out with her friends.

15. 'I _____ been a contender,' the old boxer complained.

Class/Homework exercise

- Take each of the bullet point words above and put them into full sentences. Underline the word you used. Try to use several of the words in the same sentence to make the exercise a little more challenging.

Exploring capital letters

Look at the following words that need capital letters. Rewrite the sentences that follow, adding them in:

- Any word that begins a sentence: **The** kid ran across the field.

1. it was clear that he was wrong. i could see it in his eyes.

   _____

2. why did she run away? was it something he said?

   _____

- A person's name: **Dave**, **Steven**, **Orlagh**, **Aveen**.
- A pronoun doesn't get one: him, her, it, me (apart from 'I').

3. dan, ann-marie, and garreth all went to see the scary film.

   _____

4. seán wanted her to see me. after thinking about it, i refused.

   _____

- The proper name of a place: **Dublin**, **Ireland**, **Europe**, **Earth**.
- A regular noun doesn't get one: city, country, continent, planet.

5. some people say that india is their dream country to visit. for me, it could be any place in asia.

   _____

6. the planet mars is only visible in the night sky at certain times of the year. the stars, on the other hand, are visible most nights.

   _____

- The proper name of geographical or historical terms: **Mount Everest**, the **Amazon River**, **World War** II, the **Great Hunger/Famine**.
- A regular noun doesn't get one: mountain, river, war, famine.

7. many climbers have died trying to scale the mountain, but for every mountaineer, mont blanc is the peak they want to reach.

   _____

8. when george w. bush invaded iraq, it began a new war in the middle east.

   _____

- The proper name of a product or company: **Apple**, **Samsung**, **Toyota**, **Liverpool FC**.
- A regular product doesn't get one: phone, tablet, car, football team.

9. for christmas this year, paula pleaded with her mum to buy her the latest smartphone. she was delighted to find a galaxy 10 under the tree.

_____

10. there was a lot of debate in the classroom over which was the better team. was it the toronto raptors or the golden state warriors?

_____

Class/Homework exercise

- Look over the type of capital letters shown above.
- Write two sentences using examples given in each of the bullet points above.

Exploring punctuation

Look at the following examples of punctuation and then rewrite the sentences given.

Full stops

Full stops are the most important piece of punctuation. They clearly tell the reader that you have finished saying one thing and are about to say something else.

An easy way to figure out where a full stop goes is to read the sentence out loud. Where does the thought or action change? Most of the time you will take a breath naturally when you reach a full stop.

1. Sam and Kat headed into the room and sat down they wanted to turn off the tv it was just too loud

_____

2. Martin ran in the door just as the bell rang he sat down and stared at the exam paper

_____

Speech or quotation marks

Speech (or quotation) marks go around **direct speech**. This means that you put an open speech mark (') before the exact words a person says and a closed speech mark (') after they stop speaking. The start of the quoted words gets a capital letter: **Brendan said, 'Yeah, I can do that.'**

- **Indirect speech** does not get speech marks. Only the **exact words** a person says gets them: **Brendan said that he could do that.**
- You also use speech marks if you are **quoting** a character from a text, quoting directly from a poem, or quoting from a reading comprehension.

3. Please let me in, said Mary. It's freezing out here, she continued.

_____

4. I wanted to tell her I was sorry, but I couldn't get the words out. I just mumbled, fine by me, before walking away.

_____

Commas

Commas are used in two important ways. The first is for listing things. A comma goes between every item on a list, even before 'and' (this is called a serial or Oxford comma): **I bought jam, bread, and butter at the local shop.**

- There's no need for a comma if the list has only two items: **I bought bread and jam.**

5. The four countries that finished ahead of us in the group were Italy Spain Portugal and France.

_____

6. The fireman broke down the door ran up the stairs burst through the flames and saved the little kid.

_____

The other kind of comma is to separate clauses in a sentence. Put simply, it's when you take a slight natural pause: **The use of calculators is not allowed, which is really unfair.**

- You need this kind of comma if you start a sentence with 'before', 'because', 'to' or 'as': **Before going down the stairs, I put on my dressing gown.**

7. Because of the massive rainfall the street flooded.

_____

8. To drain the road completely a huge pump had to be brought in.

_____

Question marks

Question marks are needed if you are asking a direct question. Questions usually begin with 'who', 'what', 'when', 'where', 'why', or 'how': **How are you going to get there? When will you arrive?**

- Sometimes a question is implied by the tone of the sentence: **'You want to join the team?' said Shauna. 'I didn't know that.'**
- You don't need a question mark if it's just a statement. **'I see. You want to join the team,' said Shauna. 'Then, what you need is a new kit.'**

9. What was I doing there. I wasn't sure. 'You need help,' a passer-by told me.

_____

10. I didn't know what I was doing there. 'Why am I here,' I thought. A passer-by asked me, 'You need help, buddy.'

_____

Exploring grammar

Look at the following examples of good and bad grammar. Then rewrite the sentences given.

Tenses

Switching tenses is a huge problem for many students. Make sure to keep all your sentences in the same paragraph in one tense.

- The easiest tense to write in is the **past tense**, so put the following sentences into the past tense:

1.   I ran up to him. He looks tired so I give him some air. Then I hand him a drink of water.

   _____

2.   I have enough money for my trip, so I booked my flight. I flew out the next day. I save for
     months to be able to afford the holiday.

   _____

Sentence fragments

Sentence fragments happen when you don't complete the full sentence, and it just stops midway through what you're trying to say: **Because of the way she looked at me.**

- Sometimes fragments are caused by putting full stops in the wrong places:
  I went to. Go but I couldn't.

3.   Because of his use of metaphor in his poetry. o————

   > The sentence finishes too early. Finish it off.

   _____

4.   I wish. I could go. But my mam. Won't let me.

   _____

   _____

Class/Homework exercise

- Write a paragraph of around 50 words in the past tense about a time when you went on holidays.

- When you are finished, reread it and make sure that it is all in the past tense.

- Check for sentence fragments and correct them if there are any.

COMPREHENDING

About this section: Comprehending

Lessons 3–20 will help you develop the skills you need to read and analyse questions, and structure your answers for Comprehending Questions A and B.

Planning work and sample answers on writing news reports, articles, blogs, talks, and diary entries are included in the lessons.

As in the exam, this section is organised by theme. These are:

- The world around us
- Life in the 2020s
- Achieving our goals

THE WORLD AROUND US

Learning Objectives – By the end of this lesson you should:

- Understand what makes a **speech** different to other ways of communicating
- Be able to analyse the **questions**
- Be able to **plan** and **write** coherent answers

 Time to Think

A **speech** or a **talk** is different to written communication. A speech is addressed to a crowd of people who are standing right in front of you. How is a letter or a novel different? During a speech, some people will agree with you and some won't. How does this affect what you say?

Have you ever given a speech? How did you feel making it?

Can you think of any famous speeches from history, sports, or films?

How can you tell if a crowd likes or loathes a speech?

Before you read …

Do you know anything about the Black Lives Matter movement or Alicia Garza? If you don't, research the names online and then discuss what you find out with your class.

Question analysis

Here is a step-by-step guide to answering questions in the **Comprehending** section of the exam. You will need to go back and forth quite a bit when analysing the **text**.

CARPA

C – Context – read the context

A – Analyse – read and analyse the questions

R – Read – read and analyse the text – underline direct quotes and references

P – Plan – plan your answers

A – Answer – answer the questions

Step 1: Read the context (C)

At the beginning of each text there is a section that outlines where the extract comes from, who the writer of the text is, and what the text is about. This is valuable information as it is unlikely that you will have ever seen the text before. Why should you read this first?

Comprehending A

Step 2: Read and analyse the questions (A)

Next, you should skip to the questions that follow the text.

Read the questions and underline the **key question words**. Look for:

- **Parameters to the question** – Are you only allowed use certain paragraphs?

- **The number of ideas needed** – Does it give you a specific instruction, such as, 'Give three reasons'? Also look at the number of marks for the question. You need **one full paragraph** for every **5 marks**.

- **Author or you?** – Is the question asking for the author's opinion or yours?

- **Other key question words** – These give you hints as to what to look for when reading the text.

Step 3: Read the text and analyse the image (R)

Now it's time to read the text carefully and **underline any references** you can use in your answers. Also, note down what strikes you as important about any **images** shown with the text. There are further tips for analysing images in **Lesson 4** (page 21).

Step 4: Plan your answers (P)

Once you've finished reading and analysing the text, plan out the questions. Why is this important to do? Some questions about the following text already have **ideas** to get your planning started.

Step 5: Answer the questions (A)

Now that you've read the **context** (C), **analysed** the questions (A), **read** the underlined the text (R), and **planned** your answers (P), you can now **answer** the *questions fully (A)*. Follow the **IRE** paragraph structure and make sure to have an introduction and a conclusion.

> Bookmark the CARPA steps on this page so that you can refer back to them as you work through each lesson.

Tip For Success

Stating ideas

Every answer you write will require you to express **ideas**, use **references** from the text, and **explain** your points (**IRE**). The trick is to be clear without repeating yourself. **Linking** your ideas is very important, but the examiner would get tired of reading 'My first point is …', 'My second point is …', 'My third point is …' pretty quickly.

Use some of the sample phrases below to link your ideas:

- Firstly, …

- In addition to this, …

- Another point would be …

- Leading on from this, …

- Another similar point is …

- My second point …

- In contrast to my last point, …

- This juxtaposes with …

- This continues in …

C – Read the context to the question.

WHY BLACK LIVES MATTER

The following is an edited extract from a speech made by Alicia Garza, one of the founders of the Black Lives Matter movement, at the Citizen University Annual National Conference in the US. In it, she speaks about the reasons why the campaign is needed, and what she hopes it will achieve.

1. It's great to be here. Thank you so much for having me. It is important to us that we understand that movements are not begun by any one person. <u>That this movement actually was begun in 1619 when black people were brought here in chains and at the bottoms of boats</u>. With that being said, our role has been to remind us of our humanity. To remind us that black lives matter, too. To remind us that we are still living in a time when that is a contested statement. And it should not be.

R – Read and analyse text and images.
Underline direct quotes and references for use in your answer.
Reference to Q (i) – examples of racism.

2. When I was in high school, I was required to take a civics [CSPE] class where I learned about my responsibilities as a citizen of the United States. My civics class taught me about how our system of democracy works. It taught me about where that system of democracy comes from, and it taught me that citizenship was a privilege earned only by active participation. And yet what civics did *not* teach me, and black people *like* me, was that my citizenship is conditional. This is the harsh reality for black people in America today.

3. In 2005 [after Hurricane Katrina], black people – many of them poor – waved white T-shirts on tops of roofs in the Gulf Coast, waiting for relief that still today has never come. Stuffed in stadiums, abandoned in jails, shot as we were attempting to cross bridges to find safety, we were called looters and rioters while white families were called finders and survivors.

4. In 2009, Oscar Grant was shot at a BART [railway] station platform [by a BART police officer] just three blocks from my home on New Year's Day. In 2012, Jordan Davis was executed in Jacksonville, Florida for being guilty of playing his music too loud in a gas station. In 2013, 19-year-old Renisha McBride was shot when she went onto the porch of a man that she didn't know after she had gotten into a car accident, asking for help. She was shot through a locked security door. In 2014, 12-year-old <u>Tamir Rice was shot and killed by police officers</u> in Cleveland while playing alone in a park.

5. We've been living in an era where everything and nothing is about race. Where expectations of the events that I just described are often cast aside as the result of a few bad apples, or an unfortunate consequence of what happens to people who don't try hard enough to succeed.

6. Each year, there are more than one thousand fatal shootings that occur by on-duty police officers. Each year, less than five of those shootings result in a charge of murder or manslaughter against those officers. The solution to police violence and police brutality is not to lock up killer cops. The solution is to reimagine what kind of safety do we want and deserve.

7. Even still, even though it's not enough, and even though it is not the solution, those convictions would not have happened <u>were it not for the organizing and disruptions of the last few years</u>. Were it not for the organizing that didn't get national attention, prosecutor Timothy McGinty, who refused to bring charges against the officers who killed 12-year-old Tamir Rice playing alone in the park, would still have a job.

> **R – Read** and analyse text and images.
> Reference to Q (ii) – can protesting change the world.

8. You see, black people, black resistance, and black organizing, has changed the landscape of what is politically possible. Whether or not you call it Black Lives Matter, whether or not you put a hashtag in front of it, whether or not you call it The Movement for Black Lives, all of that is irrelevant. Because there was resistance *before* Black Lives Matter, and there will be resistance *after* Black Lives Matter.

9. I believe deeply in our ability to succeed. <u>I believe deeply in our creativity, in our courage, in our determination.</u> Let us build the movement that says, 'Not in our name.' Let us build the movement that unites millions of us, brilliant and wise in our differences, and convicted in the belief that we are exactly what we need to free ourselves.

> **R – Read** and analyse text and images.
> Reference to Q (iii) (b) – Garza as a passionate speaker.

Symbol:
Alicia Garza with a determined face

Symbolises:
She is prepared to fight for what she believes in.

Symbol:
Sign saying: *Demilitarise the police*

Symbolises:
Shows people think the police act too much like the army.

Symbol:
Women holding a *Black Lives Matter* sign

Symbolises:
_____
_____
_____

IMAGE 3:1

For sample answers to question (i) below, see the **Sample answer** in the **Introduction** section of this workbook (page vii).

A – **Read** and **analyse** the questions.
Remember: (1) parameters; (2) number of ideas; (3) author or you? (4) key question words.

Question B – 50 marks

(i) Based on your reading of the first four paragraphs, outline three examples of racism shown toward Black people in America given by the speaker. Support your answer with reference to the text. (15)

A – **Answer** the question using IRE: Idea, Reference, Explain.

1. It says Black people were brought to America in chains.

2. _____

3. _____

P – Plan your answers.

(ii) Do you believe that protesting is a good way to change the world? Give reasons for your answer. (15)

1. Protesting shows governments that many people feel strongly about something.

2. _____

3. _____

Tip For Success

Exam focus:

Question (ii) above doesn't say your **ideas** have to come from the text. You can come up with your own ideas. Questions that don't ask you about the text directly come up often in the exam.

(iii) (a) In your opinion, what message is being conveyed by IMAGE 3:1? Support your answer with reference to IMAGE 3:1. (10)

1. Alicia Garza is a strong woman who is proud of her culture.

2. _____

(b) 'Alicia Garza is a passionate speaker who is very convincing.' Give reasons why you support or do not support this assessment. (10)

1. She gives many shocking examples of racism.

2. _____

Learning Objectives – By the end of this lesson you should:

- Be able to identify the **audience** and **register** for a talk or speech
- Know the **structure** of a talk or speech
- Be able to **plan** and **write** a 500-word answer for a Comprehending B question

Time to Think

There are many occasions in life when we have to stand up in front of a group of people and speak: a best-man's wedding speech or a presentation to co-workers in an office, for example. Can you think of any others?

Whatever the situation, there are two vital things to remember: the **audience** and the **register**. Why is it vital to figure out **who** you are speaking to (**audience**)? How will knowing this influence the way you speak?

Here's an example from US President John F. Kennedy's inauguration speech (the ceremony where he became president in 1961):

> 'And so, my fellow Americans: ask not what your country can do for you – ask what you can do for your country.'

Who is he **addressing** in this speech? What **tone** has he taken? Is it the right one for the situation?

Remember to think about the **audience** and **register** when you are writing a speech or talk.

Definition

Register: is the way you speak and the kind of words you use. If you are speaking to your friends, you would use an **informal** register. If you are giving an important presentation to the board of directors in a big company, you would use a **formal** register.

PCLM

P – You must be able to show the examiner that you know what a **talk** is. You must also show that you realise you are being listened to by a group of people, and that you understand who your **audience** is.

L – The language of **persuasion**, **information**, and **argument** are key here.

Exploring a talk

Being able to write a **speech** or a **talk** is an important skill, and it is one that students will have worked on during CBA1 in Second Year. The structure for writing a speech or talk is similar to every other Question B form of writing, but it is vital that it addresses the key fact that you are speaking to an **audience** as much as possible.

Here is a sample paragraph about why you would be an excellent Student Council leader (2012 exam question). In groups, read the sample and answer the questions that follow.

Malala Yousafzai gives a talk after receiving the Leadership in Civil Society award at the annual Clinton Global Initiative award ceremony in 2013.

It is well known that inclusiveness is hugely important in our school. Many of you here today were involved in Respect Week, which I helped organise. The school came together as one to show everyone here that, no matter where you're from, what religion you are, what colour your skin is, and, yes, even who you fancy, you are respected. We are an inclusive school, and one I'd be proud to be the voice of.

(75 words)

Remember

Remember IRE: As you read the sample paragraph, put an 'I' beside the **idea** that is stated, an 'R' beside the **reference** to back up the idea, and an 'E' beside the **explanation**.

1. Who is the **audience**?

   _____

2. What **register** is used?

   _____

3. Which part of the text shows us that this is a **speech**?

   _____

Tip For Success

Symbol and symbolises

Just like the Junior Cycle final assessment, you will be asked to analyse images in Paper I of the Leaving Certificate exam.

There are usually one or two small images, or one large one, beside each text. The easiest way to unpack an image is to look for symbols in the picture, such as objects or facial expressions, and try to figure out their deeper meaning. For example, in the image shown below, the manager on the left-hand side of the picture is a symbol, and he symbolises instruction, motivation, and planning. There are many images throughout this book, so use the **Symbols and symbolises** technique with each of them.

Question analysis

Symbols and symbolises: *Football manager Jürgen Klopp gives a team talk. How do you think the match is going? What do you think he is saying to the players?*

Note

In the B questions in the Comprehending section, you may be asked to write a **talk**. In the Composing section, the exam often asks for a **speech**. Your **speech** will need to be longer and more detailed as there are more marks in the Composing section, and often the **tone** is more **formal**.

Now look at the following question from 2017. The **words in bold** are important as they tell you what kind of question it is. The last line is also important because it tells you what you need to include in your answer.

Question B – 50 marks

Students can benefit from advice when choosing which subjects to do for their Leaving Certificate course. Your school principal has asked you to give a **talk** to Third Year students who are about to choose their Senior Cycle subjects. In your talk, you should explain to the students why it is important to make good decisions when choosing subjects for their Leaving Certificate and suggest what you think they should consider when making these decisions.

1. Who is the **audience**?

   _____

2. What **register** should you use?

   _____

3. Reread the question, and number the things you need to include in your answer. (Hint: Look for commas and the word 'and', especially near the end of a question.)

We now need to look at **structure** and **planning**. You must include:

Structure – Talk

An introduction	**The main body of the answer**	**A conclusion**
• An **engaging opening line** to grab the audience's attention.	• **Seven to eight** planned IRE paragraphs of about 70 words each.	• **Recap** all the main points made.
• Say who you are and why you are there to speak.	• They can be individual paragraphs or grouped into sections.	• Remind the audience who you are and why you are there to speak.
• **Outline** (but not explain) what you are going to speak about.	• You must **link** them to add to your coherence mark.	• Finish with a **statement** that makes the audience remember you.

A 50-mark question is quite a long one, which is why is it so important to know what you're going to talk about before you start writing. When you first looked at the question above, you should have noted that there are **two** parts to it. Both of them need roughly **four** paragraphs of information. Plan out what you will speak about in each one.

1. Explain to the students why it is important to make good decisions when choosing subjects for their Leaving Certificate.

    a. *The Leaving Cert is the quickest way to get the career you want. If you do well in it, then you can get into the course or trade you desire straight away.*

    b. _____

        _____

    c. _____

        _____

    d. _____

        _____

2. Suggest what you think students should consider when making these decisions.

    a. *If you want to do a particular subject in college, then you should definitely sign up to do it for Leaving Cert.*

    b. _____

        _____

    c. _____

        _____

    d. _____

        _____

✍ Time to Write

Now that the **planning** is completed, we can start to write out the answer. The first part is the **introduction**. Finish the **introduction** below with help from the prompts.

> Say why they should listen to you. How will it benefit them?

Let's face it, you're only fifteen, and you're being told to make important decisions about your future. I get it. It's rough. But _____

_____

_____

I am Alex O'Callaghan, a 6th Year at this school, and I am here to talk to you fine people today about _____

_____

_____

> In just one sentence, say why you are there.

The first thing that I am going to talk about is _____
_____
_____
_____

Then I'm going to give you tips on _____
_____
_____
_____

For each of the **main body** paragraphs, you should follow the **IRE** approach.

If you want to do a particular subject in college, then you should
definitely sign up to do it for the Leaving Cert. For example, if you want to be _____
_____
_____
_____
_____

So, choosing this subject will help massively because _____
_____
_____
_____
_____
_____

Once you have finished your point, remember to **refer** to the question as this will enhance your **purpose** mark.

> This is why it's so important to think of what you want to do after school before you pick your subjects.

Try to vary your vocabulary at the end of each paragraph so it doesn't get repetitive. Finally, raise your **coherence** mark by linking your paragraphs together using phrases and words like these at the start of the next paragraph:

> Another thing to consider is …
>
> Once you've looked at this, then …

Now it's time for the **conclusion** (which is really just the reverse of the introduction).

Quickly recap some of the points you made.

Overall, it's so important that _____

_____

_____

I am _____

Say who you are and why you've been speaking.

_____

_____

_____

_____

Finally, let me leave you with this _____

Leave the audience with a question or a statement to think about.

_____

_____

_____

_____

_____

_____

Time to Finish

With your answer planned and some sample paragraphs done, it's now time to complete your answer on a separate page.

 Time to Impress

A **talk** or a **speech** is an interactive experience. It's up to you to be creative in adding **audience interaction** into your speech. Here are two ideas about to how to do it:

Question from the audience

A lady in the front row just asked me ...

Sinéad wants to know what I think about ...

Can you think of another way of showing **audience interaction**?

Here's another way to bring in the ideas of the audience:

Show of hands and then comment

Raise your hand if you've ever ... That number is way more than/about /far below what I expected ...

> ## Class/Homework exercise
>
> - Read and analyse the questions below.
> - Then, plan out your answers.
> - Finally, write full 50-mark answers.
>
> 1. Your school is in the final of a major sporting event. You are the coach of the school's team and at half-time your team is losing. Write the **talk** you would give to inspire the team's performance in the second half of the match. (2015)
> 2. Write the text of a **talk** that you would give at a happy family event in which you recall some of your important family memories. (2013)
> 3. Imagine you are running for election as leader of the student council in your school. Write the **talk** you would deliver to your school assembly outlining the qualities you feel you possess that would make you an excellent leader of the student council. (2012)

 Time to Reflect

1. Why should you work out who the **audience** is?
2. How can you decide which **register** is best to use in a talk or speech?
3. What is the best way to identify the number of parts in a question?
4. Is it important to plan out the paragraphs in advance? Why?
5. How can you bring audience interaction into your **talk** or **speech**?

LESSON 5: COMPREHENDING A – NEWS REPORT – THE BIG FREEZE

Learning Objectives – By the end of this lesson you should:

- Understand what makes a **news report** different to other ways of communicating
- Be able to analyse the **Comprehension** questions and the **news report** itself
- Be able to **plan** and **write** coherent answers

 ## Time to Think

A **news report** tells us about something that has happened. It describes in detail an event that people want to know about. Whether a report is newsworthy depends on the **audience**. What do you think most people will want to hear about? A wildfire or last night's match? An earthquake or a celebrity's love life?

What do you think are the biggest stories in the news today?

Do you generally hear the writer's opinion in a news report or headline?

Before you read …

Have you experienced a big weather event, such as a storm, in your life? How did it affect you?

How would the closing of an airport affect people?

Question analysis

To prepare your answers, remember **CARPA** (Context, Analyse, Read, Plan, Answer) from **Lesson 3** (pages 15–16).

Tip For Success

Selecting information

It is crucial to choose which **information** from the text is important for answering the questions. The key thing is to **analyse** the questions carefully first. They will give you the **keywords** you need to find the information.

For example, the first question in the Storm Emma text on page 28 asks what the airport crews had to do to *prepare for the storm*. This means that any time you see an example of storm preparation, you must underline or highlight it. Think of words that are **similar** to 'prepare', like 'planning' or 'plan'. Also, look for words that describe what happens if you're not prepared, such as 'caught short'.

NEWS REPORT ON THE IMPACT OF STORM EMMA, 2018

The following is an edited news report by journalist Paul Hosford for the news website, TheJournal.ie. It is about the clear-up of snow from Dublin Airport after Storm Emma in 2018.

WORKING 12-HOUR DAYS AND MOVING 400,000 TONNES OF SNOW – HOW DUBLIN AIRPORT CREWS OVERCAME THE BEAST

1. As airlines worked to put stranded passengers on flights yesterday, they did so with planes taking off near a massive snow pile. That pile was the culmination of a week's work by crews at Dublin Airport, who worked around the clock to ensure that the airport remained open throughout the storm that battered Ireland last week.

2. Ice is a major problem for airports as it is essential that aircraft have enough braking action to allow them to stop safely on a runway when moving at speed. A build-up of snow or ice on a runway can dramatically reduce the available friction required for braking, making it unsafe for aircraft.

3. For Ian Devine, the Head of Asset Care and Delivery with Dublin Airport, that meant lessons had been learned nearly a decade ago. 'The snow and ice event we had in 2010–2011 led to a significant investment in equipment, staff and contractor resources, including a €5 million spend on equipment.

4. 'Now, for 20 weeks across winter, we have an action plan that means contractors are ready to respond within an hour, which means we were well placed to clear the airfield. The plan really kicked in as it was designed to.'

5. That plan led to 100 on-site staff and 200 contractors working to clear the nearly 1,000-acre site (400 landside and 600 airfield). That meant serious planning and long days for staff.

6. Devine said, 'We had been monitoring it all weekend, but when we got the forecast on Monday, we put teams on 12-hour 7 a.m.–7 p.m. shift cycles. Teams were split in two and when one crew stopped at 7 p.m., another took over. It meant we had to book a lot of accommodation in local hotels and had to look at areas within the airport to set up makeshift accommodation. We had people sleeping in the airport to make sure we weren't caught short.'

7. Devine says he is pleased with the attitudes of staff. 'The morale and the community spirit in the airport really showed itself. The commitment to go above and beyond was exceptional. I've been here 15 years and have never seen anything like it. I don't know if it was adrenaline or what, but it was amazing. I was here four days straight and nobody wilted. We kept everything open as much as possible and at no point were pavements contaminated.'

8. That work means that there are now massive snow piles in parts of the airport. After ploughing, the snow is transported via a convoy of trucks to specific designated areas on remote parts of the airfield where the drainage is carefully managed as part of the overall pollution control system.

9. That is the next challenge for Devine's team. '[We have] well in excess of 400,000 tonnes of snow. It's not thawing that fast so we will have to keep an eye on localised flooding and bring in pumps where necessary.'

10. However, that doesn't mean they are taking any time off, with the summer flight season right around the corner, when 41 airlines will move up to 740 times a day, carrying around 75,000 passengers daily. 'There's no time to think about it, really. We've had meetings all morning – it's now time to deal with the aftermath and deal with the summer schedule.'

Read and analyse the text and images.

IMAGE 5:1

Symbol: Aeroplane covered in ice
Symbolises: Danger that it might not be able to fly correctly.

Symbol: Snow ploughed into a big pile
Symbolises: ___

Symbol: Darkness and floodlights
Symbolises: ___

Read and analyse the questions.

(i) Based on your reading of the news report, what has Ian Devine had to do to prepare for Storm Emma and to keep the airport open during it? Explain your answer with reference to the text. (15)

1. _____

   _____

2. _____

   _____

   Plan your answers.

3. _____

   _____

(ii) Which of the following word or words do you think best describes the news report shown?
1: Informative   2: Interesting   3: Boring.
Explain your answer, supporting the points you make with reference to the text. (15)

1. _____

   _____

2. _____

   _____

3. _____

   _____

(a) How does IMAGE 5:1 show the hard work that Ian Devine's crew put in? Support your answer with reference to IMAGE 5:1. (10)

1. _____

   Answer the question using IRE.

2. _____

(b) 'News reports should only give the news in a balanced and factual way. They should avoid showing the views of the author.' Give reasons why you support or do not support this assessment. (10)

1. _____

2. _____

Comprehending A

LESSON 6: COMPREHENDING B – NEWS REPORT

Learning Objectives – By the end of this lesson you should:

- Understand how a **report** is different from an **article** or a **blog**
- Know what needs to be included in a **report**
- Be able to **plan** and **write** a 500-word answer for a Comprehending B question

 Time to Think

You might have heard the term 'fake news' over the last few years. This refers to news reports that do not report news accurately or which show bias, but it can also be used as a term to attack factual stories that reflect badly on a person. To write a good news report, you have to present the news in a clear way that tells the reader what happened, why it happened, and what else will happen because of it. In other words, a news report needs to be **factual** and **informative**.

> **Definition**
>
> **Bias**: means that you prefer one side over the other. You are not being fair and equal to both sides.

When was the last time you read the news? How was it delivered to you? Did it contain any opinion or bias? Was the register formal or informal?

The most reliable style of news report is written in **broadsheet** style. In a broadsheet article, the language is quite formal with no slang. It's important when you write a news report that you are not emotional or one-sided. Look at this example:

What are these images telling us? Do they show bias? How do you think they portray Trump and Clinton?

Trump wins presidency, defeats Clinton in historic election upset

Donald Trump, defying the pundits and polls to the end, defeated Hillary Clinton in Tuesday's presidential election and claimed an establishment-stunning victory that exposes the depth of voter dissatisfaction ... The first-time candidate once dismissed by the political elite will become the 45th president, Fox News projects.

Source: Fox News Channel

Which news site wrote this article? Do you think they support Trump or are they against him? Are they objective? It's often hard to keep our own views silent in a **news report**, but you must report only the facts and leave the opinion and personal experiences for **articles** and **blogs**.

PCLM

P – You need to demonstrate that you know how a **news report** is different from an article or blog.

L – Reports **explain** and **describe**, so they use the language of **information** and the language of **narration**.

Tip For Success

Timing in the exam

You have **170 minutes** in Paper I to answer questions worth 200 marks. Here is one way to manage your timing to ensure that you finish the paper:

Take roughly **10 minutes** to look at the general theme of the exam (written on the first page of the paper), read the context for each of the three texts, look at all the questions, and view the Composition titles.

Always **choose the Question B that suits you best** first. Then choose the **Question A**. Finally, decide which **Composition** question you are going to do.

Spend roughly **45 minutes** completing Question A. This includes reading the text and planning your answers to the four questions.

Spend roughly **40 minutes** on Question B. This includes time to plan your answer.

Then spend roughly **65 minutes** on the Composition question. This also includes planning time.

That leaves **10 minutes** at the end to go through your answers to make sure you've answered everything. If you stick to the timing, you may have left some answers short. Leaving this time at the end gives you some space to finish them off.

You can answer the questions in any order you like; just make sure to label them very clearly for the examiner.

Exploring a news report

Here is the question that appeared in the 2016 exam. In groups, read the sample and answer the questions that follow.

> Imagine that you are a journalist in 1916. Based on the diary extracts below, write a **newspaper article**, either broadsheet or tabloid, in which you report on the events that took place in Dublin between 24 and 29 April, 1916.

The fighting began on the morning of Monday, 24 April, when rebels began taking over several key buildings in Dublin city centre, including the GPO and Jacob's Biscuit Factory. They held off the army forces for a time before reinforcements arrived two days later, on Wednesday. The fighting became intense at this point, and there were many killed and injured on both sides.

(63 words)

Note

Be careful! This question asks for a **'newspaper article ... in which you report on the events'**. That tells you it should be written like a report and not an article where you give your *opinion*.

1.   Does this report show bias? _____

2. Write down **three facts** given in the paragraph:

a. _____

b. _____

c. _____

Question analysis

Now that we have a better understanding of what a news report should read like, we can now analyse a sample question and plan out an answer.

A major snow storm has just hit Ireland. Most of the country is under at least a foot of snow. You are a reporter for a broadsheet news site, and you've been asked to write a **news report** on the impact of the storm. In it you should describe what happened, talk about how people were affected, and explain what will happen next.

1. What will your report be about? _____

2. Reread the last line and mark the number of things you are being asked to do in your report.

The **structure** of a news **report** is different to the other styles of functional writing. It will still have an **introduction**, **main body paragraphs**, and a **conclusion**, but there are certain things that need to be included.

Structure – News Report

An introduction

- Write a **headline** that suits a **broadsheet**: A headline needs to grab the reader's attention, and it needs to be clear, descriptive, and factual.
- Write the reporter's name and the date.
- **Sum up** the entire story in two to three sentences.

The main body of the answer

- **Seven to eight** planned IRE paragraphs of about 70 words each.
- You will need paragraphs with:
  - Detailed **descriptions** of what happened (3 to 4 paragraphs).
  - **Background information** on the event (1 to 2 paragraphs).
  - **Eyewitness accounts** from people who were there (1 to 2 paragraphs).
  - An **expert** who gives their opinion on the event (1 to 2 paragraphs).

A conclusion

- Quickly recap what happened.
- Outline what is going to happen next. If you don't know, make a guess using the information you have written so far.

RTÉ reporter Teresa Mannion making her infamous 'unnecessary journeys' report during Storm Desmond in 2015.

Now you understand what is needed in your **structure**, you can plan out your answer.

What happened during the storm?

1. *It snowed for ten hours, leaving cities under three feet of snow.*

2. _____

How were people affected by the storm?

1. *Some people were trapped and couldn't leave their cars and houses.*

2. _____

What are the government and county councils doing to clear the snow? What is the weather due to be like for the next few days?

1. *More snow is expected. But not as bad as yesterday.*

2. _____

 **Time to Write**

Now that the plan is done, it's time to write your **introduction**.

Snow Hits Ireland, Leaving Many Stranded in Their Homes
or
Snow Storm Smashes Ireland

> Which of these headlines suits the **broadsheet** style?

Reporter: April O'Neill   25 March 2020

A massive snow storm has hit Ireland over the last 24 hours, causing _____

_____

_____

_____

_____

_____

_____

> Write down two to three results of the storm. You don't have to describe them yet.

For the **main body paragraphs**, it is very important to describe what happened in as much detail as possible. You need to do this for about **three to four** paragraphs. The language of **information** is key here.

Just detail for how long and how heavy it was snowing.

A snow storm lasting for ten hours hit Ireland yesterday, causing mayhem across the country.
It began snowing yesterday at _____

_____

How cold was it? How were people affected?

Temperatures fell to _____

_____

It is still snowing today, but/and _____

_____

Are things getting better or worse?

_____

Also, try to add in some **background details**. Has anything like this ever happened before? You are allowed to make it up.

This kind of snow hasn't been seen since _____

_____

You will then need to add in **eyewitness accounts** and **expert opinion**. Look at the **Time to Impress** section (page 35) to learn how to do that.

Finally, you need to have a **conclusion**. Simply sum up what happened and say what will happen next.

Briefly recap the story.

So Ireland has been hit hard by _____

_____

The weather is due to improve/get worse, so the government hopes _____

_____

_____

What is due to happen next? Will the roads be reopened? Will the snow melt?

 Time to Finish

With your answer planned and some sample paragraphs done, it's now time to complete your answer on a separate page.

Time to Impress

Eyewitness accounts and expert opinion

It is important for your **news report** to look as genuine as possible. To do this, you must add in quotes from people who were involved in the event. Remember to add in quotation (or speech) marks around the exact words the person said.

First, give an **eyewitness account** of someone who was affected by the storm:

1. Mrs Tina Caulfield of Athenry, Co. Galway, was stranded for five hours when her car was snowed in. She said, 'It was awful. I didn't think I'd survive.'

2. Michael Dooley from Dublin 6 said that _____

_____

Next, write down an **expert opinion**. For example, from a Garda official, a member of the fire brigade, or someone who represents the government.

1. Shauna Brady, spokesperson for the Minister of Transport, said, 'We hope to have all major roads open, but local roads are still very dangerous.'

2. Sam Baines, spokesman for Dublin Fire Brigade, said, _____

_____

Class/Homework exercise

- Read and analyse the following questions.
- Then plan out your answers.
- Finally, write full 50-mark answers.

1. You have attended a major sporting event (like the All-Ireland final) or cultural event (like the MTV European Music Awards) as a reporter for the *Irish Times*. Write a **newspaper report** on the event focusing on what happened in the lead-up to the event, what occurred during the event, and the celebrations afterwards. (Sample)

2. The *New York Times* has created a website for young people all around the world who want to be journalists and reporters. They say they will publish the best **newspaper reports** that are sent in about an important local event. Write a report about an event in your area (for example, a charity fun run, or local sporting rivalry) that includes background about the event, what happened during the event, and how the event impacts on the local area. (Sample)

Time to Reflect

1. How is a **news report** different to an **article** or a **blog**?
2. What is **bias**?
3. What is broadsheet style?
4. What kind of **register** should you use in a **report**?
5. What is a **headline** designed to do?
6. What do eyewitness accounts and expert opinions add to a news report?

Learning Objectives – By the end of this lesson you should:

- Understand what makes a **diary entry** different to other ways of communicating
- Be able to analyse the questions and the diary itself
- Be able to **plan** and **write** coherent answers

 Time to Think

What makes a diary entry unique is the **audience**: who it is written for. Normally, when we write something, we write it to be read by someone else; for example, homework is read by your teacher, or a business report is read by your boss. But how is a diary different? Who is the audience for a diary entry? Because of this unique aspect, the tone of a diary is a lot more personal and honest.

Can you think of any famous diaries?

Have you ever read someone else's diary?

Before you read …

Do you use Twitter? What are the positives and negatives of this social media platform?

What is your understanding of the term 'the Troubles' in Northern Ireland?

Question analysis

Now prepare and plan your answer using **CARPA** (Context, Analyse, Read, Plan, Answer) from **Lesson 3** (pages 15–16).

TWITTER DIARY – NORTHERN IRELAND IN 1981

The following are diary entries from a week in the life of a 13-year-old girl living in Northern Ireland in July 1981. In them, she describes the world she is growing up in. The author of the diary has now created a Twitter account where she tweets out what she wrote in the diary back in 1981.

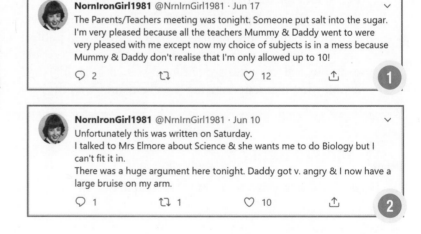

Lesson 7: Diary

NornIronGirl1981 @NrnIrnGirl1981 · Jul 15
Written on Sunday. From what I remember of today we went to Quinnsworth & I got a "Pop Diary" to keep a list of the charts. Me, Tony, Ethna took the dogs for a walk to Albert College. Pepsi lost his lead.
💬 1   🔁   ♡ 5   ⬆️   **3**

> Pepsi is the name of her dog.

NornIronGirl1981 @NrnIrnGirl1981 · Jul 16
We went into town. It was very uneventful. I got the top 20 in my dairy but it wasn't easy. We went for a great drive to Phoenix Park & right out to near Drogheda. On the way back we called in for some Kentucky Fried Chicken. It was gorgeous. We got chips as well.
💬   🔁   ♡ 11   ⬆️   **4**

NornIronGirl1981 @NrnIrnGirl1981 · Jul 16
Top 20, 16 July 1981
💬 2   🔁   ♡ 12   ⬆️   **5**

NornIronGirl1981 @NrnIrnGirl1981 · Jun 22
A policeman (Catholic) was shot dead in the Bridge Bar on Trevor Hill. Ethna & I went down to see. We met Catherine who was going to have her hair cut & Daddy gave us money to get ice-cream. Ethna & I went to meet Catherine. Her hair is lovely. Then we 3 went to confession.
💬 2   🔁 4   ♡ 22   ⬆️   **6**
Show this thread

> The INLA were a paramilitary group in Northern Ireland.

NornIronGirl1981 @NrnIrnGirl1981 · May 15
An INLA gunman was buried & a girl of only 14 yrs was buried. I think that was awful. All her school-friends line the road and many of them were crying.
So today really was a very unpleasant day in all ways.
💬   🔁 1   ♡ 23   ⬆️   **7**
Show this thread

NornIronGirl1981 @NrnIrnGirl1981 · May 13
I nearly forgot, Pope John Paul II was shot today. It was terrible. He was shot in the hand, arm & stomach by a Turk who was quite nice (God forgive me). The Pope was quite seriously hurt but will live (T God!). He lost a lot of blood.
💬 5   🔁 8   ♡ 49   ⬆️   **8**

NornIronGirl1981 @NrnIrnGirl1981 · May 14
Adam & The Ants no. 1. Madness have climbed up 2 after going down to no. 6, which is good. Spurs won the FA Cup Final 3-2 against Man. City. It was quite exciting. Villa, the Argentinian scored 2 v good goals & Crooks scored the other. The Pope is making a good recovery
💬 1   🔁 2   ♡ 20   ⬆️   **9**

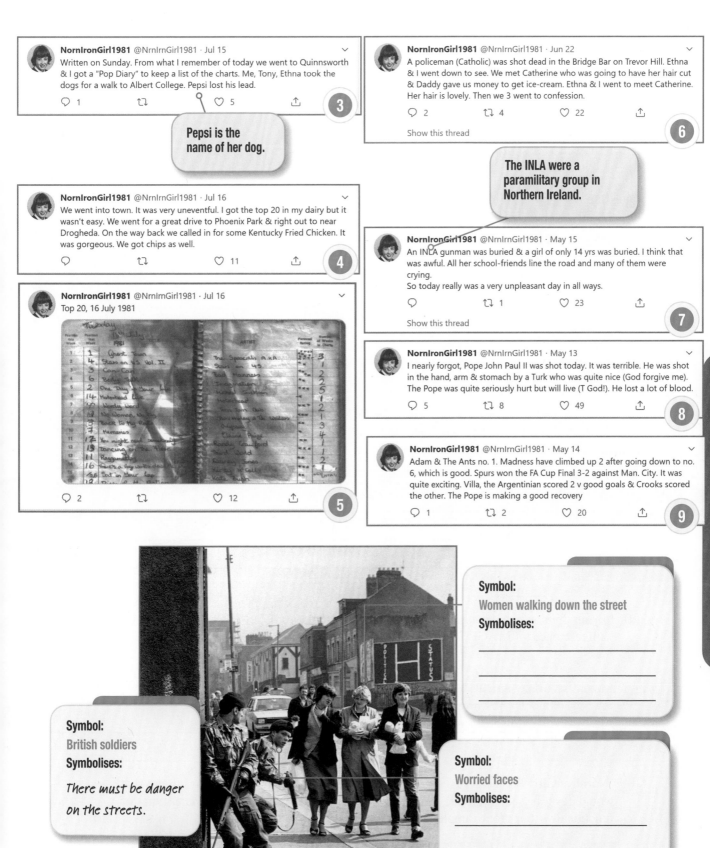

IMAGE 7:1

Symbol:
British soldiers
Symbolises:
There must be danger on the streets.

Symbol:
Women walking down the street
Symbolises:
_____
_____
_____

Symbol:
Worried faces
Symbolises:
_____
_____
_____

Giving your opinion

In the Leaving Certificate examination, you will see many questions with phrases like 'in your opinion'. To answer these questions, you need to express your own thoughts. Whatever your opinion, if you back up your idea with references to the text or image and you add an explanation (**IRE**), it is valid.

Question A – 50 marks

Based on your reading of the first six tweets, how does it show that the girl's life could be considered very normal? Explain your answer with reference to the text. (15)

1. _____

2. _____

3. _____

In tweets 4, 6, and 7, we can see how life in 1980s Northern Ireland was dangerous and sometimes deadly. Do you feel safe living in today's world? Or do you think it was safer in the past? (15)

1. _____

2. _____

3. _____

(a) In your opinion, what message is being conveyed by IMAGE 7:1? Support your answer with reference to IMAGE 7:1. (10)

1. _____

2. _____

(b) 'NornIronGirl1981's diary (shown here in tweets) is very personal and says things that would never be said out loud.' Explain how diary entries are different to other types of functional writing; for example, a personal letter. (10)

1. _____

2. _____

LESSON 8: COMPREHENDING B – DIARY ENTRIES

Learning Objectives – By the end of this lesson you should:

- Know how vital **secrecy and emotion** are in a diary entry and be able to use them in your own writing
- Be able to plan a **diary entry** question, even if it asks for a series of entries.
- Be able to **plan** and **write** a 500-word answer for a Comprehending B question

 Time to Think

Diaries are a highly personal look at ourselves and our own lives that aren't supposed to be read by anyone else. Why can we be so **secretive** in a diary entry? How does this give us the opportunity to show our **emotions**? Many people find diaries hard to write. Why do you think that is?

Here is an edited example from the diary of Kurt Cobain, the former lead singer for the band Nirvana in the early 1990s, who wrote about how he felt about fame:

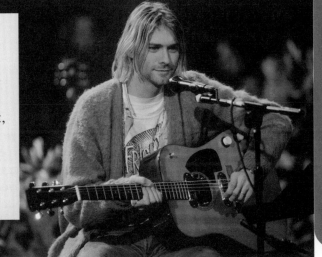

> I kind of feel like a dork writing about myself like this as if I were an American pop-rock icon or a self-confessed product of corporate-packaged rebellion. But I've heard so many insanely exaggerated stories or reports from my friends and how I'm a notoriously f—ed up heroin addict, alcoholic, self-destructive, yet sensitive, fragile, little pissant who at any minute is going to OD. Oh Pleez GAWD, I can't handle the success! And I feel so incredibly guilty for abandoning my true comrades.

Who is Cobain addressing? What freedom does this give him?

Who is the **audience** when you are writing a **diary entry**? What is the **register**?

PCLM

P – You need to understand that the audience is *you* and write in a way that shows this. Your answer needs to show secrecy and emotion.

L – Even when you use the language of narration to describe your day or the language of information to detail it, remember that it must include how you *feel* about what happened.

Exploring a diary entry

You have been writing diary entries since primary school, so you will have had a lot of practice by this time. Now, you need to look at how to improve your **diary-entry** writing skills. In groups, read the following sample paragraph and answer the questions that follow.

The preparation for the final is going well enough, I suppose. There's an awful lot of pressure on my shoulders as captain, but I can't really let that show. There are times when I'd love to just scream at the others for not pulling their weight, but what would that achieve? I want to win so badly, and I know Stan is a weak link, but it's not like I can tell him that. Sometimes I wish someone else was the leader, but, then again, I want to be the one to lift that cup up first.

(97 words)

Remember

Remember IRE: As you read the sample paragraph, put an 'I' beside the **idea** that is stated, an 'R' beside the **reference** to back up the idea, and an 'E' beside the **explanation**.

Find and underline an example of **secrecy** in the example.

Now find and underline an example of **emotion**.

Question analysis

Now look at the question from the 2018 exam below. Remember to focus on the **words in bold**, which tell you what kind of question it is, and the **last line**, which tells you exactly what you need to include in your answer.

> **Question B – 50 marks**
>
> Imagine you are representing your school in the final of a competition. You are free to choose any type of competition: sports-related, debating, singing, etc. Write **three diary entries** in which you record the details of your training or preparation for the final, reflect on the challenges you have faced during the competition, and consider what inspires you to keep working hard in advance of the final.

Anne Frank, one of the most famous diarists in history, kept a diary while in hiding during World War II before she was found and murdered by the Nazis.

1. The audience is you only, so what **register** should you use? _____

2. Reread the question and number the things that you must include in your **diary entries**.

3. You are being asked to write **three diary entries**. This means there should be **progression** in them. Think about what this would add to your answer.

Definition

Progression: means how things develop (get better or worse) over time.

'Imagine you are ...'

These kinds of questions can throw some students. You need to put yourself **in another person's shoes** and answer from their **perspective**, which is difficult in an exam situation where the pressure is on and thinking time is in short supply.

In the 2019 exam, students were asked to imagine that they recognised their tent in a photo of discarded tents at Electric Picnic. What if you've never been to the festival? What if you don't own a tent? What if you've never gone camping? All you need to do is **use your imagination**. Practise doing these questions in advance, and you will find them easier on the day of the exam.

Now we need to look at **structure** and **planning**. This is a long question, and you will need to think about your answer before you start writing. You must include:

Structure – Diary

An introduction

- Write 'Dear Diary' and the date and time. This will help show **progression**.

- Describe how you are feeling now after the day you have just had. Use the **present tense**.

- Hint at what happened but don't give it away.

The main body of the answer

- **Two to three** planned IRE paragraphs of about 70 to 80 words each.

- Keep this part in the **past tense** as you describe in detail what occurred.

- Remember to use **secrecy** and **emotion** in your writing.

A conclusion

- Outline what **could happen to you tomorrow**. Give a few possible options, and describe what the consequences might be.

- Say when you hope to write next and sign off with your initials.

The question asks for **three** diary entries, so make sure to do this **three times**.

We can now plan out what the **main body** will look like for the question:

What is the final you are training/preparing for? _____

What did you have to do for your training/preparation?

1. *Practise hard at my strengths, often for long periods of time.*

2. _____

3. _____

What challenges have you faced on your journey up to this point?

1. *Nerves nearly meant that I couldn't compete, but I overcame them.*

2. _____

3. _____

What inspires you to keep working hard going into the final?

1. *My coach's belief in me gives me confidence.*

2. _____

3. _____

The last thing you need to do is to decide on the **progression** of your diary entries. Complete the section below, filling out what will happen:

1. It's two weeks before the final. How are things going? Challenges?

    _____

    _____

2. It's a week before the final. Have things improved? Have they gotten worse?

    _____

    _____

3. It's the night before the final. How are you feeling? Do you think it will go well?

    _____

    _____

Time to Write

Now that you've completed your planning, it's time to write your answer. The introduction sets up each entry. It should be full of **emotion**.

[   ]   [   ]

Dear Diary,   1 September 2020

I honestly can't believe it. It all happened so quickly earlier. I'm still shaking.
The smile hasn't left my face since I got the news. Let me explain what happened.

[   ]

Which **emotions** are shown by the words and phrases indicated above? Fill in the boxes with your answers.

You need to show how your training and preparation is developing, whether you are writing about sports, debating, or singing.

Then it's time to flesh out one of your **ideas** using an **IRE** paragraph. Complete the section below:

> **Idea:** The sample given earlier in the plan.

> **Reference:** What were you doing during those hours? How were you training/preparing?

I had a feeling that all my hard work would pay off. All those hours of _____

_____

_____

I knew it would all work out because _____

_____

_____

> **Explain:** Why did you know it would work out? What about your training/preparation made you confident?

Don't forget to **refer to the question** and link your paragraphs for **coherence**.

Finally, you need to work on your **conclusion**. Remember to outline the possibilities.

So tomorrow we have our first proper practice before the final. It could go great if _____

_____

_____

> **What will need to happen for it to go well?**

Or it could be a disaster if _____

_____

_____

> **What dangers are there for it to not go well? Who might perform badly?**

Either way, I'll write soon and say what happened.

H.P.

 Time to Finish

With your answer planned and some sample paragraphs done, it's now time to complete your answer on a separate page.

Time to Impress

What you think and what you say

A diary shows what people are really thinking, even if they behave differently. This technique shows that you know there are some things you would like to say to people out loud, but you know you can't.

What would you really like to say to him if there were no consequences? — *Steve was terrible all day at training. Not once did he pass the ball properly. I wanted to scream at him* _____

_____

_____

What did you actually say to him? — *But, instead, I decided to say* _____

_____

Why did you say this instead of what you really wanted to say? — *because* _____

_____

_____

Class/Homework exercise

- Read and analyse the following questions.
- Then plan out your answers.
- Finally, write full 50-mark answers.

1. Write **two diary entries**, one in which you record a time when a misunderstanding arose between you and one or more of your parents or guardians, and a second one, in which you record how you clarified the misunderstanding. (2015)

2. You have won a competition entitled 'Be a Celebrity for a Day'. Write out **two diary entries** about your experience. (2009)

3. You have been captured by the enemy during a war. Write a series of **three diary entries** recounting how you were captured, the conditions where you were kept, and how you were rescued. (Sample)

 ## Time to Reflect

1. What is the **register** when you are writing a **diary entry**? Should you use very formal language?

2. Why is **secrecy** so important in a **diary entry**?

3. Why should your character show **emotion** in a diary entry?

4. How should you plan out your answer if you have to write more than one **diary entry**?

5. How does the 'what you think and what you say' technique work? How does it show both **secrecy** and **emotion**?

LESSON 9: COMPREHENDING A – ARTICLE – SOCIAL MEDIA: PARENTS AND CHILDREN

LIFE IN THE 2020s

Learning Objectives – By the end of this lesson you should:

- Understand what makes an **article** different to other ways of communicating
- Be able to analyse the questions and the **article** itself
- Be able to **plan** and **write** coherent answers

Time to Think

Articles give journalists a chance to **investigate**. Once they have the spark of the story, they then go digging. What kinds of things would a journalist do to **investigate** a story?

Why would a journalist go to all the bother of investigating a subject and writing an article?

Can you think of any famous articles or any famous journalists?

Before you read …

Do your parents/guardians have social media accounts? How do you feel about this?

How would you feel if someone posted a picture of you without your consent? What would you do if this happened?

Question analysis

To prepare your answers, remember **CARPA** (Context, Analyse, Read, Plan, Answer) from **Lesson 3** (pages 15–16).

Remember

You will need to go back and forth quite a bit when analysing the text for the **Comprehending** section of the exam paper.

SOCIAL MEDIA PARENTS AND THEIR CHILDREN

Read the context to the question.

The following is an edited version of an article by Caitlin Gibson for the *Washington Post* about parents who post pictures of their children on social media. It deals with the impact it has on the children, and what happens when they don't want their picture posted online.

GEN Z KIDS ARE THE STARS OF THEIR PARENTS' SOCIAL MEDIA – AND THEY HAVE OPINIONS ABOUT THAT

1. Alison Santighian flicks her finger over her smartphone screen, and her Facebook profile scrolls past in a blur. She is looking for a particular photo from a few days ago, a picture her 9-year-old son, Arsen, didn't want her to take.

2. 'Found it!' she says. Arsen, sitting beside her on the family's patio, peers over her shoulder. 'He looked very handsome that day,' Alison explains, and Arsen rolls his eyes. He was dressed in a dapper white suit for a piano performance, and when Alison asked him to pose for a picture that she could share with her Facebook followers, Arsen said he'd rather not. In the end, they landed on a compromise, and Arsen did strike a pose: he slumped in his seat with a piano music book tented over his face, his expression hidden.

3. There have been more negotiations like this lately, as the Santighian kids – Arsen and his 11-year-old sister, Elsa – have begun asking questions and expressing opinions when their parents decide to share a photo or personal anecdote on social media. Such conversations have become a rite of passage among families where children of a certain generation – the true digital natives, many of whom may have debuted on Facebook before exiting the womb – are now old enough to have their own ideas about what they want their online presence to look like, and who has the right to shape it.

4. At first, the choice belongs to parents alone. An infant can't object to a soft-filtered selfie with mama; a toddler won't know if their tantrum becomes a topic of online commiseration. But when, exactly, does it start to change? Is there a turning point somewhere between first steps and first school dance,

a clear moment when one's offspring becomes an independent being whose experiences belong to them, too, and not just to a proud (or frustrated) parent who just wants to boast (or ask advice, or vent)?

> **Offspring = children**

5. The stakes of this particular family conflict are poised to increase as more members of Gen Z – a generation that the Pew Research Center defines as those aged 22 and younger – come of age. Children might first be concerned about what their friends think of a parent's posts or pictures – but later, new concerns are added to the mix: if you made a joke that your dad shared on Twitter, will a college-admissions officer think it's funny? If a potential employer googles your name, would they find pictures of you and your sister in bathing suits at the beach?

6. Alison and her husband, Pete, think the line of authority begins to blur a bit as kids become teens and inch closer to legal adulthood.

For now, when Elsa and Arsen object to a photo or a social media post, they are encouraged to explain why, and Pete and Alison take those points seriously.

7. But ultimately – in this household, at least – the parents make the final decisions, and they don't have to ask permission. 'We do post things that they don't know about,' Alison says. 'Cute pictures of them sleeping, for example.'

8. 'Oh, I know about that,' Elsa corrects her. 'It's kind of creepy, if you think about it.' She smiles and shrugs. 'But I'm fine with it.'

9. 'Why is it creepy, Elsa?' her father Pete asks.

10. 'Because you're *in your sleep*,' Elsa says.

11. 'We look at you all the time when you're asleep!' Alison says.

12. 'That's *looking*,' Arsen interjects, 'not *posting*.'

13. Alison and Pete consider this for a moment. Alison laughs and starts nodding. 'You know,' Pete says, 'that's a good argument.'

> **Read and analyse text and images.**

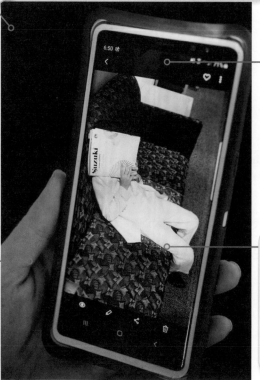

IMAGE 9:1

Symbol:
Parent's hand
Symbolises:
They take the photo and post it with a tap.

Symbol:
The mobile phone
Symbolises:
_____
_____
_____

Symbol:
_____
Symbolises:
_____
_____
_____

Question A – 50 marks

(i) Based on your reading of the article, how do the children feel about their pictures being posted online? What do the parents think of their views? Support your answer with reference to the text. (15)

1. _____

2. _____

3. _____

(ii) With social media and the internet, young people are recording their lives like never before. Do you think this is a positive or a negative development? Explain your answer. (15)

1. _____

2. _____

3. _____

(iii) (a) Imagine you are the child in IMAGE 9:1. Write a note to your parents explaining how you feel about them taking the picture and that they posted it. Support your answer with reference to IMAGE 9:1. (10)

1. _____

2. _____

(iii) (b) 'Articles which investigate important issues are really important to society.' Do you think it is important for journalists to investigate big news stories and powerful people? Explain why you think this. (10)

1. _____

2. _____

Tip For Success

Presenting the evidence

When we read an article, the writer **presents** the evidence to us. Sometimes they give their own opinion on what's going on, but most of the time they will present the information to the reader and let them make up their own minds. Louis Theroux, the well-known documentary maker, is famous for this style: he speaks to the people in the documentary, asks them simple questions, and shows us the responses without much commentary.

In this **article**, we see this style quite clearly. The first question asks about how the **children feel** and what the **parents think** about their views. It doesn't ask for the writer's opinion. You have to look at the evidence the author presents, think about it, and then come up with your own conclusions.

LESSON 10: COMPREHENDING B – ARTICLE

Learning Objectives – By the end of this lesson you should:

- Understand what an **article** is and how it is different to a report
- Know what you need to include in an **article** and the **tone** needed
- Be able to **plan** and **write** a 500-word answer for a Comprehending B question

 Time to Think

If a **report** provides factual information on something that has happened, how is an **article** different? In an **article,** a journalist investigates a story to give a new perspective on it. It is written for the reader to enjoy reading and to be challenged. The tone is less formal than a report and can be more descriptive.

One famous article was the *Time* magazine exposé that launched the #MeToo movement, when the women of Hollywood finally spoke up about sexual harrassment by some of the most famous producers, actors, and directors. It inspired many more women around the world to speak up too.

> The women and men who have broken their silence span all races, all income classes, all occupations and virtually all corners of the globe. They might labor in California fields, or behind the front desk at New York City's regal Plaza Hotel, or in the European Parliament. They're part of a movement that has no formal name. But now they have a voice.

Crowds protesting at a #MeToo march.

Is this **article** simply reporting what happened? Can you tell if the writer is in favour of or against the #MeToo movement? When writing an **article**, you will have to think like an investigator and a reporter.

PCLM

P – As it is an **article**, it is important to write in the correct **register**. Pay close attention to who you are writing the article for and for what **purpose**.

C – It is vital to **plan out** your answer. Carefully map out what you are going to talk about before you start writing.

Exploring an article

When you are asked to write an **article** in the Leaving Certificate, the question will ask you to explore a topic you already know about in an interesting way. You won't need to write about the latest political stories or a big celebrity scandal. In 2019 there was a question about the 'value of volunteering'. Here is a sample paragraph. Read it and, in groups, answer the questions below.

Lots of my friends ask me what I get from volunteering with my local football club. They know I give up two weeknights to train the under-10s and most of my Saturday for their match. But let me tell you, to see the delight in the kids' faces as they play ball, or the joyful looks their parents give them after the game, makes it worthwhile. Without people volunteering, Mountview Boys and Girls FC would be no more. That's why I do it, and that's why I value volunteering so much.

(91 words)

1. Does this read like a **news report**? Explain your answer.

_____

_____

2. What example of volunteering does the writer give?

_____

3. Circle the words in the paragraph above that show the positive emotions volunteering can bring.

Question analysis

Articles can come up as a 50-mark **Question B** or a 100-mark **Composition** question. The **structure** for both questions is similar except for one very important detail: you will have to write a lot more for in the 100-mark question. Analyse the question below and then plan it for 50 marks.

Tip For Success

Choosing your questions

It is vital that you **choose the right questions** in the exam. Poor decisions at the beginning can cost you valuable marks and time. That is why it is important to spend time **choosing the best Question B** for you *before* choosing a Question A. Both are worth 50 marks, but because Question B is one single task instead of four smaller questions, it must take **priority**.

The reason is simple enough. If you're good at writing an article, and it comes up, then focus on that. The same goes for any type of functional writing. If you choose the Question A first, then you could be left with a Question B that doesn't suit you or that you find difficult. Making a mess of this question can hurt your overall mark in big way. But, if you mess up an answer in Question A, you still have three more to excel in. So, in short, always choose your Question B first.

Question – 50 marks

Write an article, to be published in a popular magazine, on the value of volunteering with at least one sporting or charitable organisation. The article should discuss the possible benefits for the people who volunteer their time and energy, and for the organisation(s) involved.

> The '(s)' at the end of organisation means that the 's' is **optional**. So you could talk about one organisation or many organisations. The '(s)' gives you a choice.

1. Which magazine are you going to write for? _____

2. What organisations are you allowed to talk about volunteering for? _____

_____

3. Are you only allowed to talk about one organisation? _____

4. Reread the last line and mark the number of things you are being asked to talk about in your article.

_____

The **structure** of an **article** is similar to that of most of the Question Bs you have already worked on.

Structure – Article

An introduction

- Write a **title** that suits the topic of your article, and makes the reader want to read it. Don't make it too boring or factual.

- Give the **writer's name**.

- Open up with an interesting point or **anecdote**.

- Then outline some of the things you are going to speak about in the **article**.

The main body of the answer

- **Seven to eight** planned IRE paragraphs of about 70 words each.

- You will need paragraphs that include a **personal reflection** on the topic with some **research**.

A conclusion

- **Sum up** what you've spoken about.

- Say if you've **changed your views** on the topic.

- Leave the reader with **something to think about**.

Definition

Anecdote: a short, amusing or interesting story about a person that says something about their personality.

Once you understand what is needed in your **structure**, you can **plan** out your answer.

What are the benefits for the people who volunteer their time and energy?

1. *It makes them feel better knowing that they are supporting their community.*

2. *It gives them a chance to make new friends.*

3. _____
   _____
   _____

4. _____
   _____

What a journalist's desk might look like. Look at all the research they have to go through before they are able to write their article.

What benefits are there for the organisations?

1. *They would not be able to run without people donating their time.*

2. *It spreads the name of the organisation in the community.*

3. _____
   _____

4. _____
   _____

Note

For the 100-mark **Composition** questions, more is needed. Instead of having one paragraph on each point, you will need *two*. We will continue the plan for the 100-mark question on pages 183–184 in **Lesson 31** of the **Composition** section.

The Foróige logo. What do you think of their slogan? What do 'empowering' and 'enriching' mean?

Time to Write

Now that the plan is done, it's time to write your **introduction**.

Why I volunteer, and why you should too

By Lois Lane

Think of the child staring at a computer screen. Think of an empty football pitch. So how do we get the kid from the couch to the pitch? Well, _____

_____

_____

_____

> Say how valuable volunteers are to help children in this way.

Put simply, volunteers _____

_____

_____

_____

> Say what volunteers do for organisations and why they do it. Refer to your **plan**.

For the **main body** paragraphs, it is very important to **describe** and **explain** your point.

> Why do you think the Foróige club relies on volunteers? Why can't they afford to pay them?

So, could charitable organisations actually run without the help of volunteers? From my experience, no. These organisations, like the local Foróige club for teens in my area, rely on volunteers because _____

_____

_____

The financial value of volunteering can be seen quite well here as _____
_____
_____
_____

How can the financial value be seen? How much would it cost to pay people to organise and bring the teens on trips? Feel free to estimate the number. Just make it believable.

Finally, you need to have a **conclusion**. Sum up what you've been talking about, and say how your point of view has changed or stayed the same.

So let's be honest, volunteering is so important to organisations because _____
_____
_____

Briefly recap why it's valuable to the organisation.

But what I've found out is that it's also valuable to the person volunteering too as _____
_____
_____

Say how it can be valuable to the person volunteering too.

I'm going to leave you with this: the next time you are asked to volunteer your time, _____
_____
_____

Give advice to the person reading as to why they should volunteer.

 ## Time to Finish

With your answer planned and some sample paragraphs done, it's now time to complete your answer on a separate page.

 ## Time to Impress

Personal approach

When you write an **article**, the reader often looks for the writer's personal view on the topic. Were you shocked by what you discovered? Did it change how you feel about the topic?

The journalists Carl Bernstein and Bob Woodward (l–r), whose investigative journalism helped bring down the US president, Richard Nixon.

1. When I began looking into volunteers, I expected to see old people helping other old people. But, in reality, I was delighted to see _____

_____

_____

2. Before I spoke to parents about their use of social media, I thought they would all think it was only for young people. What I found shocked me as _____

_____

_____

3. To think, before I began my journey around Ireland visiting these places, I thought a sun holiday would be the only kind of holiday for me. But now _____

_____

_____

Class/Homework exercise

- Read and analyse the following questions.
- Then plan out your answers.
- Finally, write a full 50-mark answer.

Definition
STEM: **S**cience, **T**echnology, **E**ngineering, **M**aths

1. Write **an article** for your school's website in which you outline your own experience of any of the STEM subjects and explain why you would or would not encourage students to study these types of subjects for their Leaving Certificate. (2018)
2. With #MeToo, women in Hollywood stood up against injustice. Write **the article** that you would write for a national newspaper in which you identify an injustice about which you feel strongly, and suggest ways in which you think this injustice could be addressed or overcome. (2016)
3. Write **an article** for your school magazine or website where you investigate 'getting out of your comfort zone'. In it you could talk about your own experiences in school, the teams or clubs you joined, and what you learned about yourself by doing something different. (Sample)

 Time to Reflect

1. How is an **article** different to a **news report**?
2. What is the difference in tone between a **report** and an **article**?
3. What is the biggest **planning** difference between a 50-mark and a 100-mark question?
4. What should a headline do in your **article**?
5. Should you include personal experience in an **article**?

LESSON 11: COMPREHENDING A – BLOG – LIVING WITH AUTISM

Learning Objectives – By the end of this lesson you should:

- Know what a **blog** is and how it is different to a **diary entry**
- Be able to analyse the questions and the **blog** shown
- Be able to **plan** and **write** coherent answers

 Time to Think

Writing a **blog** is a chance to talk about yourself in a personal way but in a public medium. In a **diary entry**, you don't want people to know your business. How is a **blog** the opposite?

Do you follow any bloggers, or influencers, or YouTubers, or gamers? Who are they? Why do you follow them?

So who is a blog aimed at? The **audience** is something all bloggers have to consider when they start writing. If it is a fashion blog like Suzanne Jackson's *So Sue Me*, who will be the main target market? Other blogs are designed to take you out of your comfort zone: to show you something you think you already know in a new light, or to give an insider's view.

If you were to write a blog, what part of your life would you blog about? Why this particular aspect?

Before you read …

What comes into your mind when you think of the word 'autism'? Research the word if you are unsure of what it means.

Why is it important to learn more about illnesses, disabilities, and disorders that we don't know enough about? How can we learn about them?

Question analysis

To prepare your answers, remember **CARPA** (Context, Analyse, Read, Plan, Answer) from **Lesson 3** (pages 15–16):

LIVING WITH AUTISM

The following is an extract from the book *Can You See Me?* by authors Libby Scott and Rebecca Westcott. Libby is autistic and writes a blog about living with autism. She made her blog into a book and published it when she was 11. It aims to show people who don't have autism what life is like for someone who does. This extract is about making friends and how Libby feels about stimming.

1. Date: Friday 19th September
Situation: We're getting a dog!! (not to keep, just to borrow, but still – it's a dog!)
Anxiety Rating: 2 out of 10. Because dogs make everything better, even Dad getting angry with me and making me feel sad and horrible.
2. I'm so excited about Rupert coming to stay. I LOVE ANIMALS. They are like extra friends that don't judge you. Like, I was watching some dogs in the park yesterday and they just ran up to each other and made friends immediately. No small talk or pretending. I'm jealous of how easy they find it. I've noticed some dogs make themselves look approachable by wagging their tail to show they are friendly – I wish I could do that but I have no tail. The human way of doing this is smiling, so I try and do that when I remember.

---

3. What else do dogs do to make friends? Oh yes, they sniff each others' rear ends. Maybe I should try that tomorrow. I'll just run around the playground sniffing at all the other kids' behinds. THAT should make me new friends… Ha ha ha, just kidding!

4. Animals get misunderstood just like I do. I was watching *The Cat Goes Or I Do* this morning with these terribly behaved cats. It turns out they're just anxious and misunderstood, and when the owners stop punishing them for their bad behaviour and start treating them differently, with more understanding, and just kindness really, they behave so much better. Teachers should watch more programmes like that. Just saying.

5. Libby's autism facts: Stimming

Pro: Stimming is a kind of coping mechanism for me. It's when I make movements or sounds, or fiddle. For ages I didn't even know it was called stimming or that a lot of autistic people do it to help themselves feel better. There are good stims that don't do any harm – like beatboxing, which is actually something I need to do because it helps me concentrate. When I'm stressed I do a flappy, clappy thing with my hands – but sometimes I do that when I'm excited too.

Con: The con to stimming is mainly that other people don't usually like me doing it. It irritates or embarrasses them, and they seem to think I'm doing it just to annoy them. Some teachers get so shouty about me humming or fidgeting or whatever, that they make me stressed and want to stim even more – especially because I know I can't.

6. That's when I go to Plan B, which is bad stims. They're more subtle, so other people are less likely to notice them. Biting nails, picking skin, pinching myself, that sort of thing. People don't seem to mind these as much, which is weird because they're much more harmful to me. I get really sore fingers, bruises and other marks all over my skin.

7. I once lost my middle finger nail on my left hand from picking at the skin around my fingers, which led to an infection, which made my nail go black. The doctor said I could have got sepsis which can be fatal. So I reckon that basically means some people might unknowingly cause you to die of a terrible infection rather than let you do a bit of harmless humming or tapping. In other words, STIMMING SAVES LIVES.

8. Actually, the more I think about it, the more I reckon that a lot of the cons of autism are not really caused by autism but by how other people react to it. I really do.

IMAGE 11:2

Symbol:
'Expected to fit in. Proud to stand out'

Symbolises:
Shows how people want her to just 'be normal', but that is not her.

Symbol:
Jigsaw pieces that are a symbol for autism

Symbolises:
_____
_____
_____

LIBBY SCOTT & REBECCA WEST

CAN YOU SEE ME?

IMAGE 11:1

Symbol:
The image is of a figure standing on a roof with their arms open

Symbolises:
_____
_____

Multi-part questions

One thing that you need to be aware of is that some questions have more than one part. For 15 marks here, you are being asked what causes Libby stress, *and* how she relieves the anxiety. It can be very easy in an exam to miss the second part and only answer the first. If you do, you will be marked down, even if the answer is brilliant. Make sure you give at least **one paragraph** to **each part** of the question.

Question A – 50 marks

(i)   From your reading of the blog, what causes Libby anxiety? What does she do to relieve
      her stress? Support your answer with reference to the text.   (15)

1. _____

2. _____

3. _____

(ii) It can be hard to put yourself in someone else's shoes. In this blog, Libby puts you in
      the shoes of a person with autism. Apart from a blog, outline three other ways you could
      learn about a topic from a different viewpoint.   (15)

1. _____

2. _____

3. _____

(iii) (a) Do you think IMAGE 11:1 is good cover for this book? Explain your reasons with
          reference to IMAGE 11:1.   (10)

1. _____

2. _____

      (b) Look at IMAGE 11:2. Why do you think the jigsaw puzzle piece is a symbol for autism?
          Do you think it is a good symbol to use? Explain your answer.   (10)

1. _____

2. _____

Lesson 11: Blog

LESSON 12: COMPREHENDING B – BLOG

Learning Objectives – By the end of this lesson you should:

- Know why openness and honesty are important in **blog** writing
- Understand why someone would write a blog
- Be able to **plan** and **write** a 500-word answer for a Comprehending B question

 Time to Think

A good **blog** will talk about how a person feels about events in their life. A good blogger needs to make an emotional attachment with the reader. So why is simply listing out the things you've done on holiday not enough for a travel blog? Or listing the clothes you wear not enough for a fashion blog?

One famous blogger is called the Secret Footballer. In his blog for the *Guardian* newspaper online, he gives a behind-the-scenes look at what it is like to be a Premier League player:

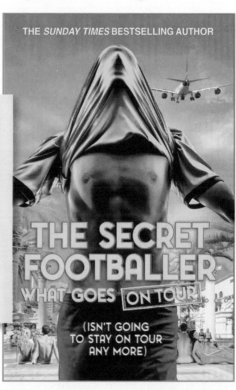

THE *SUNDAY TIMES* BESTSELLING AUTHOR

THE SECRET FOOTBALLER
WHAT GOES ON TOUR
(ISN'T GOING TO STAY ON TOUR ANY MORE)

The fans work all the hours that God sends so that they can spend part of their income on an expensive ticket to watch us play for the sum total of 90 minutes, and most of them aren't overly bothered about any problems that a player may have outside of those 90 minutes. In fact, most of the fans I talk to, including many of my friends, believe that the right amount of money will remove any problem a footballer may have. While it is true that monetary problems are generally squashed in the womb, many of the other problems everybody has to deal with in everyday life persist. We're not all that different.

What point is the blogger making about the fans?

Do they care about a player when they're not on the field?

Pick out a part where the writer shows real honesty.

The Secret Footballer, a former Premier League player, turned his blog about life in the top division into a series of books. What about this blog might interest you? What would turn you off it?

PCLM

P – A **blog** is designed to **inform** and shed new light on things, so make sure you do this when you write a blog post.

L – You need to write in an open and honest way using the language of **argument**, **information and persuasion**. Make sure to keep your readers entertained as well as open their minds to a **new point of view**.

Exploring a blog

In groups, look at the sample paragraph below from the 2019 question on recycling plastic, and answer the questions that follow it.

Let me be the first to say that recycling can be a bit of a pain. Cleaning out the bottle, carrying it around with you, and bringing it to a recycling centre – all for a whole 10 cent. You have to wonder if it's worth it. But by doing this, you can help save the planet we live on. Only yesterday, it was reported in the news that plastic has been found 350 kilometres out to sea and two kilometres deep. We are in a crisis and this scheme can only help.

(92 words)

1. Give an example where the blog writer shows honesty.

   _____

   _____

2. What kind of language is the writer using? Explain your choice.

   _____

   _____

Question analysis

Now look at the exam question from 2019. The most important parts will be **words in bold** as they tell you what kind of question it is, and **the last line** which tells you what you need to include in your answer.

> **Question B – 50 marks**
>
> You would like to establish a deposit refund scheme for plastic items such as cups and bottles in your school or workplace. People would be paid 20 cent for each cup and 10 cent for each bottle returned for recycling. Write **a post for your school or workplace blog** in which you outline your proposed scheme and encourage people to support your proposal.

1. You have a choice of **audience**. Before you continue, choose which one you are going to write for.

   _____

2. Reread the last line and number the things that you must include in your **blog**.

Now we need to look at **structure** and **planning**. It is a long question, and you will need to think about your answer before you start writing. You must include:

Structure – Blog

An introduction

- Write a **title** or **headline**, to get the reader's attention. It can be smart, funny, or informative.

- Write your name and title; for example 'Mary Martin, Student Council President'.

- Get the **audience's** attention by opening with an interesting story or idea.

- Outline who you are, and what you are going to talk about.

The main body of the answer

- **Seven to eight** planned IRE paragraphs of about 70 to 80 words each.

- Remember to be **open** and **honest** in your writing.

A conclusion

- **Sum up** the points you've made in your blog.

- Leave the reader with **something to think about**, like a quote, or a statistic, or a heartfelt feeling about the subject you've been writing about.

Ireland's most famous fashion blogger is Suzanne Jackson. Her blogger name is So Sue Me. What do you know about this blogger?

So we can now plan out what the **main body paragraphs** will look like for our question:

Who is the **audience?** _____

Outline of the proposed scheme:

1. *When you buy anything plastic in the canteen, a recycling cost will be added.*

    > **Why will you add the 10 cent on bottles and 20 cent on cups?**

2. *This is done because* _____

    _____

3. *When you bring it back,* _____

    _____

    > **What will happen when you return the plastic?**

Give reasons to encourage people to support your scheme.

1. *Stop plastic from going into the ocean.*

2. _____

3. _____

4. _____

5. _____

Time to Write

Now that you've completed your planning, it's time to write your answer. The **introduction** sets up your blog. It should engage the reader right from the start and be open and honest.

> What is your job title? Are you doing the school or workplace question?

Recycle Plastic and Save (the Earth)

> Be honest about a time you threw plastic away.

By Jason O'Brien, _____

How many times have you thrown away plastic? Just think about it. Just last week, I _____
_____
_____

But now I'm a changed person, a new man, and I'm writing today to tell you about a new plastic deposit refund scheme I want to introduce here. If you _____
_____
_____

> Very briefly, outline the scheme.

This will mean that _____
_____
_____

> Very briefly, outline why people should participate in it.

Then it's time to flesh out one of your **ideas** using an **IRE** paragraph. Complete the section below:

So firstly, how will this all work? Well, instead of paying €1.50 for a bottle of your favourite lunchtime beverage, you'll now pay _____
_____
_____

> How much will they pay now? This is to show you read the question correctly!

This isn't a huge amount of money. Like, what could 10 cent buy you? _____

_____

_____

We will keep the money. For now. This is to _____

_____

_____

Don't forget to **refer** to the question and **link** your paragraphs for **coherence**.

Finally, you need to write your **conclusion**.

So my proposal is simple: _____

_____

_____

I know it's a small step, but let's face it, if we don't change our recycling habits now, then

_____

_____

🏁 Time to Finish

With your answer planned and some sample paragraphs done, it's now time to complete your answer on a separate page.

🏃 Time to Impress

Be honest

The words 'honest' and 'open' have been used quite a bit in this lesson. If the author is **honest** and **open** about their own experience, how does that make them more trustworthy?

Here, I've cheated on a test before. I'm not proud of it. I got away with it, but the guy beside me didn't. The fear and stress it caused me – all all for a lousy C. I'm telling you, it's not worth it.

Okay, I've lied to my boss before. I told them _____

_____

_____

I felt _____

_____

_____

_____

How did you feel as you told it? What about after? Were you found out?

Listen to me, _____

_____

_____

_____

What advice would you give to people considering lying?

Class/Homework exercise

- Read and analyse the following questions.
- Then plan out your answers.
- Finally, write full 50-mark answers.

1. A travel company has employed you to visit your three favourite places in Europe and write a **blog** about your experience. In it you can talk about your journey to each of the places, what you did there, and the impact the places had on you. (Sample)

2. The company you work for has been polluting the local area and covering up the evidence. You have found out about it and know that if you tell anyone, you could lose your job, or worse. Write an anonymous **blog** where you outline the pollution your company is causing, explain how they are covering it up, and say what you hope will happen to the owners once they are found out. (Sample)

Tip For Success

'About your experience …'

Many questions in the Leaving Certificate will ask you to talk about **past experiences**. They want you to be able to write about things that have happened to you in the past in an **interesting** and **informative** way, and a blog is a perfect example of this. But what if you think your experiences aren't interesting or informative? What if you've never had the experience in the first place?

Well, you are allowed to **imagine them** and **make them up**. The examiner won't be checking the truth of what you say. A good way of doing this is to make your own experiences more **dramatic** and **exaggerate** them. You can also use experiences you have read about or seen on TV, or that have happened to your friends. Remember, the exam is testing your ability to write an answer, not your actual life.

▷◁ Time to Reflect

1. What makes a **blog** different to a diary entry?

2. Why should a blog have **openness** and **honesty**?

3. Why would people want to read a blog?

4. Where would you find a blog?

5. Why would you use **humour** in a blog?

LESSON 13: COMPREHENDING A – NOVEL – OH MY GOD, WHAT A COMPLETE AISLING

Learning Objectives – By the end of this lesson you should:

- Be able to analyse the questions and the **novel** extract shown
- Be able to **plan** and **write** coherent answers
- Be able to answer a question on **character**

 ## Time to Think

Many of us love reading **novels** and find it an engaging and rewarding experience. Over hundreds of pages, we get to know a **character**. We see them fail and succeed. We see them grow as people.

Do you enjoy reading novels?

Can you think of a novel in which there was an interesting character?

When you are given a text from a novel in the Leaving Certificate exam, you will only be given about two to three pages from it. The excerpt could be from the start, middle, or the end of the novel. You may not have seen these characters before, and the world they live in might be strange or unfamiliar. You just don't know. What problems can this cause for you?

Before you read …

Imagine you had to move from the city to the country or from the country to the city. What would be the hardest things you would have to adjust to?

What are the best and worst things about attending a wedding?

Question analysis

Read and plan your answers using **CARPA** (Context, Analyse, Read, Plan, Answer). Refer back to **Lesson 3** (pages 15–16) if you need more detail on each step.

Tip For Success

Character analysis

The first question in this text will ask you about what kind of person Aisling is. Asking for your impressions of a character often comes up as a question in the exam. Your view can be positive or negative, but, either way, you will need to support your answer (**IRE**). Think about the following questions:

- Are they nice to the other people around them?
- Do they seem intelligent or not?
- Are they afraid to say what's on their mind, or are they very outspoken?
- Do they overthink things, or do they go with the flow?
- Are they emotional, or do they bottle up their feelings?

WHAT A COMPLETE AISLING!

The following is an edited extract from the novel *Oh My God, What A Complete Aisling* by Irish authors Emer McLysaght and Sarah Breen. It is about a country girl who works in Dublin. In this excerpt, Aisling and her boyfriend, John, are having a hotel breakfast the day after a friend's wedding.

1. It's 11.25 a.m. and people are still arriving down to breakfast, heading sheepishly towards the buffet like they have all the time in the world. The staff, apparently used to this kind of carry-on, are still happily taking orders. I'm not feeling great. Of course I had the works – fresh fruit and yogurt, croissant, made-to-order omelette, *pain au chocolat*, full Irish, and about three litres of orange juice in those little thimbles that you get in hotels.

2. I catch Sinéad McGrath's eye across the room – she's tucking into a stack of pancakes like someone who's never heard of a Syn – and give her a wave. Her own wedding is less than a year away.

3. Beside me, John is horsing into the contents of his second trip to the buffet. He's always happiest when he's eating, and he looks so cute that I can't stop myself reaching out and squeezing his hand affectionately. His dark brown hair is sticking up here and there but he's pulling it off. *And* his hungover eyes are puffy. Cute as anything though. He looks up from his sausage-sandwich as I touch him and raises his eyebrows quizzically.

4. 'Nothing,' I say coyly. 'I was just thinking – imagine, this could be us in a couple of years.'

5. He raises his eyebrows a little higher.

6. 'Here, in a nice hotel, the day after a wedding,' I clarify, looking at him straight in the eye. 'Except it could be *our* wedding,' I add, glancing across at the door where the bride, clearly a bit worse for wear, is making an entrance wearing a blue and yellow Knocknamanagh Rangers jersey with 'Mrs Kelly' printed on the back above Liam's number, 8.

7. I felt a little sting of jealousy watching everyone crowd around Denise. John and I have actually been going out eight months longer than she and Liam, and they got engaged two years ago. Meanwhile, we're not even living together. It's not that I'm not happy with how thing are going – I am; it's just that I always thought they'd be going a bit quicker after being together for seven years.

8. 'Maybe more than a "couple",' John guffaws, looking back at his sausage, knocking me out of my trance.

9. 'What do you mean, more than a couple?' I ask, trying to keep my tone breezy.

10. 'Well, it's not exactly on the horizon for us, is it? I'm twenty-nine and you're only twenty-eight. You'd be a child-bride by today's standards,' he adds with a hollow laugh, spraying toast crumbs onto the shite linen table-cloth.

11. 'Denise is twenty-seven,' I reply quietly. 'She didn't do Transition Year. She thought it was only a doss and that it would get her out of the routine of studying – she actually never shut up about it...'

12. I let the words trail off and look down at my plate full of croissant crumbs so he won't see my eyes fill with tears. I can't cry here, in a room full of girls I went to school with and GAA lads. I'd never live it down. And I don't want to get into a disagreement about potentially getting married in the dining room of the Ard Rí Hotel. I haven't even showered yet.

13. 'Come on – check out is at half twelve and I want to have a wash before we go. The toiletries are Crabtree & Evelyn, I'm not missing that,' I say, standing up and throwing my napkin on the chair a little harder than I mean to.

14. At 12.31, we're pulling out of the driveway, the atmosphere between us in the car a little warmer than in the dining room, but there's still a strange tension, hanging around like a ferocious smell.

Read the **context** to the question.

A 'Syn' is a treat for people who go to Slimming World.

Read and analyse text and images.

IMAGE 13:1

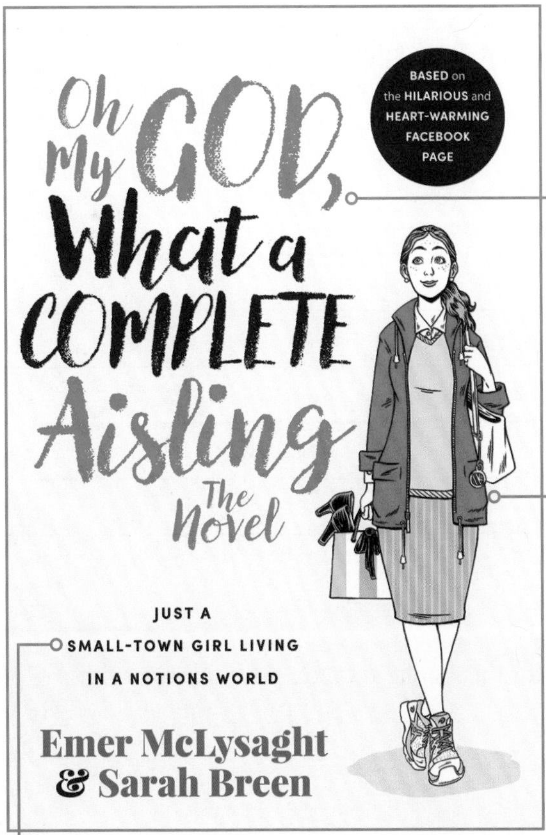

Oh My **GOD,** What a **COMPLETE** *Aisling* The Novel

BASED on the HILARIOUS and HEART-WARMING FACEBOOK PAGE

JUST A SMALL-TOWN GIRL LIVING IN A NOTIONS WORLD

Emer McLysaght & Sarah Breen

Symbol:
Sloppy handwriting font

Symbolises:
_____
_____
_____

Symbol:
Regular-looking woman with a bag of shoes

Symbolises:
This could be any young woman. Means we can relate to her.

Symbol:
'Just a small-town girl living in a notions world' to the tune of 'Don't Stop Believin''

Symbolises:
_____
_____
_____

Read and analyse the questions.

Question A – 50 marks

(i) From your reading of the novel extract, what kind of a person does Aisling come across as? Support your answer with reference to the text. (15)

Plan your answers.

1. _____
   _____

2. _____
   _____

3. _____
   _____

(ii) Which of the following word or words do you think best describes this scene?
1 – Realistic. 2 – Descriptive. 3 – Emotional. Explain your answer, supporting your points with reference to the text.

1. _____

2. _____

3. _____

(iii) (a) Do you think IMAGE 13:1 is good cover for this book? Explain your reasons with reference to IMAGE 13:1. (10)

1. _____

2. _____

(b) Imagine you are John in this scene. Write a short account of what he is thinking when Aisling mentions marriage. Refer to the text in your answer. (10)

1. _____

2. _____

Answer the question using IRE.

LESSON 14: COMPREHENDING B – DIALOGUE

Learning Objectives – By the end of this lesson you should:

- Know what **dialogue** is
- Understand that **description** is vital to good **dialogue**
- Know how to use it in an answer

 Time to Think

Writers have been trying to write good dialogue for thousands of years. How do I convey emotion in a character's words? What reaction am I looking for from the other person in the scene? How will it further my story? A good writer uses dialogue to enhance character development and to advance the storyline.

Can you think of dialogue in a film or on television that impressed you?

What makes good dialogue?

One famous piece of dialogue is from the film *A Few Good Men* in which an army general is on trial for ordering a military operation he shouldn't have.

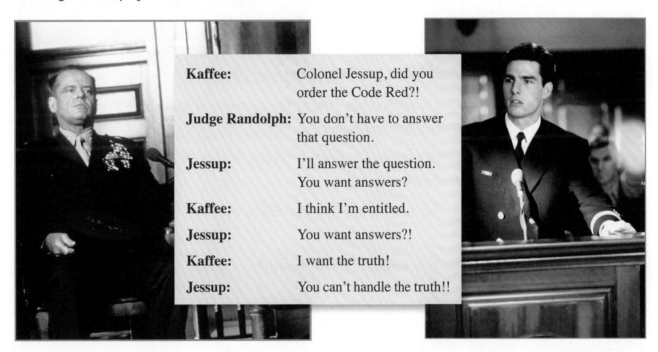

Kaffee:	Colonel Jessup, did you order the Code Red?!
Judge Randolph:	You don't have to answer that question.
Jessup:	I'll answer the question. You want answers?
Kaffee:	I think I'm entitled.
Jessup:	You want answers?!
Kaffee:	I want the truth!
Jessup:	You can't handle the truth!!

How is the emotion shown in the exchange? How do we know each person is angry or shouting? How is tension built up in the scene?

PCLM

L – Dialogue writing is a great way to include adverbs and better descriptions in your writing. Look for times when you can use an adverb to describe how a character is speaking with neutral verbs like 'said' or 'replied': **'What do you mean?' Emir replied sadly.** Look also for strong, descriptive action verbs for your dialogue tags: **'What do you mean?' Emir roared.**

M – **Paragraphing** and **speech marks** are very important when you are writing **dialogue**, so make sure you know how to use them properly.

Exploring dialogue

There are two kinds of dialogue that you will read when you are studying for your Leaving Certificate. The first is like the example from *A Few Good Men* shown on the previous page, which is from a play or a film. It will read like a script with the character's name, followed by what they say. You don't have to describe their words. It is up to the actor and the director to interpret them.

The other style is the one you will most likely use in your writing. It is the **prose** style. Here you will describe everything:

- The way the words are said.
- The body language while saying them.
- The impact the words have on the person hearing them.

Tip For Success

Better vocabulary

This lesson is all about how important **vocabulary** is. Your answers will be one in a pile of hundreds that the examiner has to correct, and many of the papers will contain answers on the same questions. Your job is to stand out.

Let's take the word 'went' as an example. This verb simply tells us that something was here and now it's over there. It doesn't say *how* it got there. Did it **stumble** or **stagger**? Did it **bound** or **rush**? Did it **creep** or **tip-toe**? Did it **storm** or **burst**? Choosing better vocabulary will really help you maximise your **language** mark.

Here is a sample answer to the 'vain and selfish generation' Question B from the 2019 paper. In groups, read the sample paragraph below and answer the questions:

I had a chat with my brother the other day. He is very into his looks and updating his Instagram page. 'Why do you do it?' I asked him, a (puzzled) look on my face.

'Well, to be honest, it makes me feel good.' He had a little smirk as he said this. 'Everyone I know has a page, and it's nice that mine gets more likes.'

My mouth was open as he said these words. 'Is that not the most vain thing anyone has ever said?' I replied, my voice high-pitched with disbelief.

'Maybe,' he said, with a shrug, 'but how many followers do you have?'

(107 words over four paragraphs)

1. What did the writer do every time someone different spoke?

   _____

   _____

2. Does this make the passage easier to read?

   _____

   _____

3. Circle the parts that describe how the words were said. The first is done for you.

4. Reread the passage again, but only the parts in speech marks.

5. Does reading it this way change the meaning of the passage?

Question analysis

You probably won't be asked to write **dialogue** on its own, but it is the kind of thing that you can add into any question, especially the Composition questions (**short story**, **personal essay**, **article**, and **speech**).

Look at the following exam questions, and describe two conversations that you could include in your answer. The first question has been done for you.

---

1. Write an article, for publication in a music magazine, in which you describe your ideas for the perfect music festival. (2019)

I could talk with a couple of my friends about what they would want to see in a music festival. I could also talk with someone who has experience running a festival to see if these ideas could work.

---

2. Write a personal essay in which you discuss what you think your life would be like if you were unable to use any form of social media for a year. (2019)

I talk with my dad about why he wants me to give up my mobile phone. After the year, I talk to him again about _____

_____

_____

_____

---

3. Write an article for your school's website in which you outline your own experience of any of the STEM (Science, Technology, Engineering, Maths) subjects. (2018)

I speak to my teacher about how hard Maths can be. I also talk to _____

_____

_____

_____

---

4. Write a diary entry in which you record the details of your training and preparation for the final of a sports event, debating competition, or song contest. (2018)

_____

_____

_____

_____

 **Time to Write**

Once you have an idea of how you are going to use **dialogue** in your work, you can then set about writing it. Here are some things to remember when you are writing **dialogue**:

- Describe how the words are said and the impact they have.

- Start a new paragraph every time someone different speaks.

- Only put **direct speech** in speech marks. **Indirect speech** doesn't need them.

Definition

Direct speech *is what the person actually says*: **'I want you to get out of my car,' John shouted**.

Indirect speech is what the person said, but not their *exact* words: **John shouted at me to get out of his car**. Have another look at **Lesson 2** if you need to refresh your memory.

Now let's work on an sample from the 'perfect music festival' question from the 2019 paper.

I called over my two best friends, Orla and Karl. I asked them what they thought should be part of a perfect music festival. `Anything you want, guys.' I grinned. `You can be as mad and out-there as you want.'

> Both **direct speech** and **indirect speech** are used in this paragraph. The **direct speech** is in speech marks. Highlight or underline the **indirect speech**.

Orla laughed and said, _____
_____
_____
_____

> What was Orla's idea? What exactly did she say? How did she say it? Use **direct speech**. Remember to include speech marks.

As she spoke, she had a look of _____
_____
_____
_____

> How did she look as she said the words? Talk about her eyes and her mouth. You can also include **body language**.

> Roughly, what ideas did he talk about? Use **indirect speech**. Make sure to explain how he spoke.

Karl's ideas were a lot different, though. He talked about _____
_____

When we were done with the interview, I thanked them. `Look, guys,' I said _____
_____
_____
_____

> What exactly did the narrator say to Orla and Karl? Describe the tone they use to show they are thankful.

 **Time to Impress**

> A verb is a doing word (running, jumping, dressing) or being word (am, was).

> An adverb is a word that describes a verb (ran <u>slowly</u>, jumped <u>high</u>, dressed <u>badly</u>).

Better verb and adverb choice

Most students use the same familiar words over and over. How can this have a negative effect on their work?

Here we are going to work on choosing better **verbs** and **adverbs** to improve your writing. Look at the sentence below:

'Give me the ball,' said Ethan.

'Said' is a **neutral** verb. It doesn't explain *how* the words were spoken. Now read the following sentences, and write in a stronger verb or add an adverb. Try to make the first example totally different to the second one to show how word choice can change the meaning.

'Give me the ball,' replied Ethan angrily.

'Give me the ball,' said Ethan sadly.

'I want it now,' moaned the child.

'I want it now,' demanded the child.

> Put a verb or adverb in the spaces provided.

'Take out your journals,' _____ *the teacher* _____

'Take out your journals,' _____ *the teacher* _____

'Believe me,' the politician _____

'Believe me,' the politician _____

Class/Homework exercise

- Go back and look at the **Question analysis** part of the lesson on page 69.
- Using the skills you have developed, write out a dialogue for each of the questions you have planned out.

A dialogue should be a communication where both sides listen and react to what the other is saying.

Time to Reflect

1. What is **dialogue**?
2. What makes good **dialogue**?
3. What do you do every time someone different speaks?
4. What is **direct speech**? Does it get speech marks?
5. What is **indirect speech**? Does it get speech marks?
6. What is a **verb**? What is a **neutral verb**? What is an **adverb**?

ACHIEVING OUR GOALS

Learning Objectives – By the end of this lesson you should:

- Understand what makes **instructions** clear and easy to follow
- Be able to analyse the questions and the **instructions** given
- Be able to **plan** and **write** coherent answers

 ## Time to Think

No one really likes being told what to do. Whether it is a teacher giving out to you, or a parent telling you what time you have to be home at, it is still an order that you have to follow or face the consequences.

Where do you typically see instructions? Think of some examples.

When it comes to instructions or advice, how do you feel when someone tries to give you some without you asking? Thankful? Annoyed? Undermined?

Instructions are different to **advice**. Advice is someone's personal opinion about what to do. But instructions give detailed information on how something works or should be done. The person following the instructions usually needs them to learn a new skill or improve a skill they already have. This means that the instructions have to be as clear and easy to follow as possible.

Before you read …

What's the best piece of advice a coach, manager, boss, or teacher has ever given you?

Has someone ever given you an instruction that you didn't follow? Why didn't you follow it? What happened afterwards?

Question analysis

Use **CARPA** (Context, Analyse, Read, Plan, Answer) to prepare and plan your answer. Refer back to **Lesson 3** (pages 15–16), if necessary.

Paralympic athlete Holly Robinson representing New Zealand in the javelin.

GOAL-SETTING AND SPORTING ACHIEVMENT

Read the context to the question.

The following is an edited article by Jack J. Lesyk, PhD, from the Ohio Center for Sport Psychology. It is about the mental skills needed by athletes to be the best they can be. It is designed for competitors at every level: from people who run for fun to professional sportspeople.

THE NINE MENTAL SKILLS OF SUCCESSFUL ATHLETES

1. You don't have to be a professional athlete or an Olympic champion to be a successful athlete. Nor do you have to have a room full of trophies, win a state championship, or make the front page of the sports section. Successful athletes that I've worked with include an 11-year-old figure skater who has not yet won a competition, a high school golfer with a zero handicap, a middle-aged runner whose goal is to complete her first marathon, a weight lifter who holds several world records, and an Olympic medallist.

2. What these athletes have in common is that their sport is important to them and they're committed to being the best that they can be within the scope of their limitations – other life commitments, finances, time, and their natural ability. They set high, realistic goals for themselves and train and play hard. They are successful because they are pursuing their goals and enjoying their sport. Their sport participation enriches their lives, and they believe that what they get back is worth what they put into their sport.

3. There are nine specific mental skills that contribute to success in sports. They are all learned and can be improved with instruction and practice.

4. Here is a detailed description of the nine skills:

i.   Choose and maintain a positive attitude
Successful athletes:
- Choose an attitude that is mostly positive.
- View their sport as an opportunity to compete against themselves and learn from their successes and failures.
- Pursue excellence, not perfection, and realise that they, as well as their coaches, teammates, officials, and others are not perfect.

ii.   Maintain a high level of self-motivation
Successful athletes:
- Are able to persist through difficult tasks and difficult times, even when the rewards and benefits are not immediately forthcoming.
- Realize that many of the benefits come from their participation, not the outcome.

iii.   Set high, realistic goals
Successful athletes:
- Set long-term and short-term goals that are realistic, measurable, and time-oriented.
- Are highly committed to their goals and to carrying out the daily demands of their training programs.

iv.   Deal effectively with people
Successful athletes:
- Realize that they are part of a larger system that includes their families, friends, teammates, coaches, and others.
- When appropriate, communicate their thoughts, feelings, and needs to these people and listen to them as well.

v.   Use positive self-talk
Successful athletes:
- Maintain their self-confidence during difficult times with realistic, positive self-talk.
- Use self-talk to regulate thoughts, feelings and behaviours during competition.

vi.   Use positive mental imagery
Successful athletes:
- Prepare themselves for competition by imagining themselves performing well in competition.
- Use imagery during competition to prepare for action and recover from errors and poor performances.

vii.   Manage anxiety effectively
Successful athletes:
- Accept anxiety as part of sport.
- Realize that some degree of anxiety can help them perform well.
- Know how to reduce anxiety when it becomes too strong, without losing their intensity.

Read and analyse text and images.

viii.   Manage their emotions effectively
Successful athletes:
- Accept strong emotions such as excitement, anger, and disappointment as part of the sport experience.
- Are able to use these emotions to improve, rather than interfere with high-level performance.

ix.   Maintain concentration
Successful athletes:
- Know what they must pay attention to during each game or sport situation.
- Are able to regain their focus when concentration is lost during competition.

Comprehending A

Symbol:

World Cup trophy

Symbolises:

Excellence. They are the best in the world.

IMAGE 15:1

IMAGE 15:2

Symbol:
Smile, with hands raised

Symbolises:

_____

_____

_____

Symbol:
Thousands of runners in the 2018 Dublin Marathon

Symbolises:

_____

_____

_____

Read and **analyse** the questions.

Question A – 50 marks

(i)   Based on your reading of the article, which three of the mental skills do you think are the
      most important to sporting success? Explain your answer with reference to the text.   (15)

1.   _____

2.   _____

3.   _____

Plan your answers.

(ii) Do you believe it is just as important to experience failure as it is to experience success?
      Explain your reasons, describing what we can learn from both failure and success.   (15)

1.   _____

2.   _____

3.   _____

(iii) (a) Describe how IMAGE 15:1 shows success. Refer to the image in your answer. (10)

1. _____

2. _____

(b) 20,000 people ran in the Dublin Marathon in 2018. IMAGE 15:2 shows some of them. Is IMAGE 15:1 or IMAGE 15:2 better at showing success? Refer to both images in your answer. (10)

1. _____

2. _____

Answer the question using IRE.

Tip For Success

Explaining your idea (IRE)

According to the last Chief Examiner's Report for English in 2013, the average mark in the Comprehending Question A in the exam is O3; for Question B, it is an O4. The big failing for students is not fully explaining the point they are trying to make.

Once you've stated your idea and given your reference, you must expand your answer and spend time explaining it. In other words, tell the reader why your idea makes sense. Explain how your reference is a good example.

If you get stuck, one trick is to explain the line you just wrote. *'Imagining success before you try means that you are thinking positively.'* Now explain thinking positively: '**When we think positively, we are in a *better mindset* to achieve success.**' What happens if we don't have a better mindset? '**Without this, we will only think of failure and won't *believe in ourselves*.**' Then explain 'believe in ourselves' and so on.

LESSON 16: COMPREHENDING B – IINSTRUCTIONS

Learning Objectives – By the end of this lesson you should:

- Know the correct **register** and **tone** needed for **instructions**
- Be able to write **instructions** that are clear and easy to follow
- Be able to **plan** and **write** a 500-word answer for a Comprehending B question

Time to Think

Instructions are strange things. They are necessary to complete many tasks in life, but very few people like following them. If you buy something from Ikea, chances are that you will try to put it together yourself before even looking at the diagrams. And, of course, there is the male stereotype of not wanting to take directions when driving. Why do you think people would rather get lost than ask for **instructions** on how to get to where they want to go?

When was the last time you read a set of instructions? What were they for?

How would you describe the tone they were written in?

Whatever your feelings on instructions, they need to be clear and easy to follow. Here are some laboratory safety instructions from the New Jersey Institute of Technology:

THINK SAFETY.
Work deliberately and carefully. No horseplay.

KNOW THE HAZARDS OF ANY MATERIALS OR MACHINERY YOU ARE WORKING WITH.
The laboratory manual and/or instructor will review specific safety issues on individual experiments before you perform any tests.

ALL STUDENTS MUST WEAR APPROPRIATE SAFETY EQUIPMENT.
Safety goggles must be worn anytime any laboratory experiment is being performed. Additional safety equipment must be utilised based on specific experiment requirements.

A typical impression of work in a lab. Are some of the instructions given by NJIT being followed?

Are these instructions clear? Are they easy to follow? How would you describe the tone of the instructions? Do you think instructions need to be so aggressive?

PCLM

P – You need to understand what **instructions** are designed to do and make sure that yours fit what the question has asked of you.

L – The **language** should be clear and simple. The **instructions** should be easy to follow (language of **information**) with reasons why they are needed (language of **argument**).

Exploring instructions

As a student, you are well used to taking instructions. So what would make you more likely to follow them? The person instructing you? The **tone** in which they are given? How clear and simple they are? In groups, look at the following sample **instructions** on how to relieve stress during your exam year, and answer the questions.

The most important thing to relieve stress is to leave the books alone for twenty minutes when things get a bit much. I'm not talking about giving up studying and homework. What I'm trying to get across is how a little thing like taking a walk or playing Mario Kart can clear your head. Then you can get back into it. You'll be surprised how something so simple can lower your anxiety.

(72 words)

Some instructions, like this set from Ikea, don't use words. Can you work out what each one is telling the customer?

1. Do you think the **instruction** given in the first sentence is clear? Why?

   _____

2. What examples are given to show how to follow the instruction?

   _____

   _____

3. What **tone** is used? Is it friendly or strict? Why does this make you more likely to follow the instruction?

   _____

   _____

Question analysis

Instructions have shown up as a part of other questions, such as the Article Question B in the 2019 exam paper:

Question B – 50 marks

You have been asked by a mobile phone company to produce **an article for their website**, offering guidance on the polite and appropriate use of mobile phones by people of all ages. The article should include a combination of 'dos and don'ts' in relation to polite and appropriate mobile phone usage. Write the article you would produce.

> For information on writing articles, go to Lessons 9 and 10.

1. Who is the **audience** for an **article** like this? _____

2. What do you think 'polite and appropriate use of mobile phones' means?

   _____

   _____

3. Circle the part of the question that shows that it is looking for **instructions**.

Now we need to look at **structure** and **planning**. It is a long question and you will need to think about your answer before you start writing. You must include:

Structure – Instructions

An introduction

- You will need a clear **heading** that sets out what the instructions are for.

- Set out some of the problems that the readers might be having with the topic, like 'Do you find studying tough?' or 'Are you nervous to get behind the wheel?'

- Say how following these **instructions** will help you succeed.

The main body of the answer

- **Seven to eight** planned **IRE paragraphs** of about 70 words each.

- Be clear with your **instructions** and explain why they are needed.

A conclusion

- **Remind** the reader what the problem was.

- Then finally say how the **problem should be fixed** now if they continue to **follow your instructions**.

So, for the question we looked at earlier, we can now plan out what the **main body** will look like. There are **two** things that you are being asked to do so you need to plan them separately.

What are the 'dos' of polite mobile phone use?

1. *Wait until you are on your own before swiping through your feed.*

2. _____

3. _____

4. _____

What are the 'don'ts' of polite mobile phone use?

1. *You don't need to share everything. Only put up and forward on things that are important. Don't overdo it.*

2. _____

3. _____

4. _____

Time to Write

Once you have finished your planning, you can now start working on writing your answer. You must set out the reasons for your instructions in your **introduction** and set the right **tone**.

Give an example of what someone does on their phone that annoys you.

How to use your phone right and be polite

Think of all those times people on their phones annoyed you. They could be _____

_____

_____

Or else they are _____

Give another example.

_____

_____

Are you one of these people? If so, these dos and don'ts are here to _____

_____

_____

What will following these **instructions** do for you?

The **main body** paragraphs follow the same structure as the sample given earlier. Remember to use the **IRE** approach and to **link** your ideas.

The biggest issue many people have about mobile phones is that they ruin conversations. Think of the last time when _____

Give an example of when you were in a group having fun.

_____

_____

Everyone is chatting and having fun, except for _____

Now say what that one person is doing. Are they on their phone? Are they paying attention?

_____

_____

_____

This is so impolite because _____

Why is this impolite?

_____

_____

_____

So make sure you only use your phone for browsing when you're on your own.

For your **conclusion**, you have to sum up what the problems were and remind your reader that now they have to tools to fix them.

Is this student using her mobile phone in a 'polite' or 'appropriate' way? What advice would you give her?

Recap some of the 'don'ts' you spoke about earlier in your plan.

So before you read these instructions you may have _____

_____

_____

How should you behave on your phone now? Make sure to use the question **keywords**.

But now you have the tools to be _____

_____

_____

🏁 Time to Finish

With your answer planned and some sample paragraphs done, it's now time to complete your answer on a separate page.

Tip For Success

Don't wander off-topic – stick to the point

Everything you write has to have a **purpose**. If you wander off into telling a story or a long description of something, you are probably not answering the question. This is a huge mistake that many students make when it comes to writing answers in the Leaving Certificate. If you ramble on and don't link what you are saying back to the question, it will hurt your **purpose** mark.

For example, if you're supposed to be explaining how you can make your school more accessible for students with disabilities, and instead you give the history of your school or a day in the life of a student, then you are **writing off-topic**. You've missed the point. Make sure to **link all points** that you make **back to the question** and avoid giving information for no reason.

🏃 Time to Impress

Showing a bad example

A key ingredient to good **instructions** is to explain what will happen if the reader doesn't follow them. Why can this be effective in making people follow an instruction?

So what happens if you don't put the phone away when in company? Well, quite simply, people will get a bit annoyed. Do you want to be known as the rude one, who won't take part in a conversation and would rather stare at a screen?

Let's say you decide to watch a YouTube video on the bus without earphones. What will people think of you? _____

_____

_____

So you're the person who answers work emails at the dinner table. You know what people think of you? _____

_____

Class/Homework exercise

- Read and analyse the following questions.
- Then plan out your answers.
- Finally, write full 50-mark answers.

1. Nujeen Mustafa, a Syrian refugee who fled to Germany from war-torn Aleppo in a wheelchair pushed by her sister, Nasri, was not able to go to school in Syria because of the difficulties posed by her physical disability. Write **an article for your school website or magazine** in which you suggest what your school could do to make the school building more suitable and the school community more welcoming for students with physical disabilities. (2017)

> Write a list of **instructions** as part of your **article** to help make the school and students more welcoming to students with disabilities.

2. Write an **article**, to appear either in your school magazine or on your school's website, in which you offer advice to your fellow students on finding a part-time job for the summer holidays. Your advice should include tips about where to find work, how to make a successful application, and how to prepare for an interview. (2016)

> Again, write your **article** using a list of **instructions** for each part of the question.

 ## Time to Reflect

1. Why is it important for **instructions** to be **clear** and **easy to follow**?
2. What **tone** should you use when writing instructions?
3. What is the **purpose** of giving a **bad example**?

Learning Objectives – By the end of this lesson you should:

- Know how an **open letter** is different to a formal letter or speech
- Be able to analyse the questions and the **open letter** shown
- Be able to **plan** and **write** coherent answers

 Time to Think

When someone in a position of power does or says something that we don't like, we have a few options open to us as to how we respond. We could write them an email, or a letter saying how unhappy we are. Does the person have to respond?

Why would someone write an **open letter**?

Have you ever read an open letter? Have you ever written one?

An **open letter** is public. You are still writing to the person, but you are publishing it in a newspaper or reading it aloud on TV for everyone to hear. How does this make it harder for them to ignore you? Also, the people who read the letter and hear your words will now put pressure on that person to reply to you.

Before you read …

What is climate change? Why is it so important to tackle it? Do you try to be 'green'?

What do you know about Greta Thunberg? Google her and the School Strike for Climate protest to find out more.

Question analysis

Use **CARPA** (Context, Analyse, Read, Plan, Answer) to read the text and prepare your answer.

GOALS TO COMBAT CLIMATE CHANGE

> Read the context to the question.

The following is an edited speech, adapted here as an open letter, published on the *Guardian* newspaper website, from Greta Thunberg to MPs in the British Parliament in April 2019. In it, she talks about climate change, and why school students are going on strike to force the people in power to do something about it. Greta is a teenage activist from Sweden.

'YOU DID NOT ACT IN TIME.'

1. My name is Greta Thunberg. I am 16 years old. I come from Sweden. And I speak on behalf of future generations. I know many of you don't want to listen to us – you say we are just children. But we're only repeating the message of the united climate science community. Many of you appear concerned that we are wasting valuable lesson time, but I assure you we will go back to school the moment you start listening to science and give us a future. Is that really too much to ask?

2. In the year 2030, I will be 26 years old. My little sister Beata will be 23. Just like many of your own children or grandchildren. That is a great age, we have been told. When you have all of your life ahead of you. But I am not so sure it will be that great for us.

3. I was fortunate to be born in a time and place where everyone told us to dream big; I could become whatever I wanted to. I could live wherever I wanted to. People like me had everything we needed and more. Things our grandparents could not even dream of. We had everything we could ever wish for and yet now we may have nothing. Now we probably don't even have a future any more.

Read and analyse the text and images.

4. Because that future was sold so that a small number of people could make unimaginable amounts of money. It was stolen from us every time you said that the sky was the limit, and that you only live once. You lied to us. You gave us false hope. You told us that the future was something to look forward to. And the saddest thing is that most children are not even aware of the fate that awaits us. We will not understand it until it's too late. And yet we are the lucky ones. Those who will be affected the hardest are already suffering the consequences. But their voices are not heard.

5. Around the year 2030, 10 years, 252 days, and 10 hours away from now, we will be in a position where we set off an irreversible chain reaction beyond human control, that will most likely lead to the end of our civilisation as we know it. That is unless in that time, permanent and never-seen-before changes in all aspects of society have taken place, including a reduction of CO_2 emissions by at least 50 per cent.

6. Furthermore, these calculations do not include unforeseen tipping points like the extremely powerful methane gas escaping from the rapidly thawing Arctic. Nor do these scientific calculations include already locked-in warming hidden by toxic air pollution. We must also bear in mind that these are just calculations. Estimations. That means that these 'points of no return' may occur a bit sooner or later than 2030.

7. No one can know for sure. We can, however, be certain that they will occur approximately in these timeframes, because these calculations are not opinions or wild guesses. These projections are backed up by scientific facts, concluded by all nations through the IPCC. Nearly every single major national scientific body around the world unreservedly supports the work and findings of the IPCC.

The IPCC is the Intergovernmental Panel on Climate Change.

8. We children are not sacrificing our education and our childhood for you to tell us what you consider is politically possible in the society that you have created. We have not taken to the streets for you to take selfies with us and tell us that you really admire what we do. We children are doing this to wake the adults up. We children are doing this for you to put your differences aside and start acting as you would in a crisis. We children are doing this because we want our hopes and dreams back.

IMAGE 17:1

IMAGE 17:2

Symbol:

Greta Thunberg – teenage climate change activist

Symbolises:

Young people making a difference.

Symbol:

Sign with the Swedish for 'School Strike for Climate' on it

Symbolises:

_____

_____

_____

Symbol:

Irish students with a thermometer sign

Symbolises:

_____

_____

_____

Tip For Success

Do you believe?

Many exam questions start with 'Do you believe?' Instead of asking you for your opinion of the text or a character, it will give you a statement like, 'Do you believe you are fortunate or unfortunate to live in an age when social media is extremely popular?' (2019 exam) You then have to **give your views** on it.

'Believe' is a very **personal** word. It means that your answer must be personal to you. Use evidence from your own life and examples you have seen around you to prove your ideas. Once you back up what you are saying and explain it in detail, your answer is valid.

> Read and **analyse** the questions.

Question A – 50 marks

(i) From your reading of the article, outline three problems Greta Thunberg sees for her generation both now and in the future. Support your answer with reference to the text. (15)

1. _____

2. _____

3. _____

(ii) Greta Thunberg has had a lot of people dismiss her points simply because of her age. Do you believe that your opinion as a teenager counts? Explain your reasons and give examples. (15)

1. _____

2. _____

3. _____

Plan your answers.

(iii) (a) What do both IMAGE 17:1 and IMAGE 17:2 tell us about the School Strike for Climate protests? Refer to both images in your answer. (10)

1. _____

2. _____

Answer the question using IRE.

(b) Your class has decided to go on the School Strike for Climate protest and have elected you to write a note to your principal explaining why you are striking. Write the note that would be delivered to the school. (10)

1. _____

2. _____

Learning Objectives – By the end of this lesson you should:

- Know the **structure** of a **letter**
- Understand that there are different types of letters
- Be able to **plan** and **write** a 500-word answer for a Comprehending B question

 Time to Think

In a world of instant communication, the idea of sitting down and putting pen to paper, then finding an envelope, stamp, and postbox, can seem weird. But letters are still very important.

In what situations would you send or receive letters?

Have you ever received or written a handwritten letter?

In what situations would you send a typed, formal letter?

Open letters, for example, can have a big impact. Unlike the rapid war of words that can take place on Twitter, when a writer pens an **open letter**, they need to think long and deeply about where they stand on a topic and come up with good arguments to back their statements and opinions. But like a Twitter tweet, an open letter is designed to be public. As your argument is going public, why do your ideas have to be strong and well backed-up?

Here is an edited extract from an **open letter** by Siegfried Sassoon, a British World War I soldier and poet that some of you may have studied during Junior Cycle. It was written in 1917, and published in *The Times*. In it, he talks about the leaders of the war:

kept going

freedom

> I am making this statement as an act of defiance of military authority because I believe that the war is being deliberately prolonged by those who have the power to end it. I am a soldier, convinced that I am acting on behalf of soldiers. I believe that the war upon which I entered as a war of defence and liberation has now become a war of aggression and conquest. I have seen and endured the sufferings of the troops for ends which I believe to be evil and unjust.

Anti-war poet Siegfried Sassoon who experienced the horror of fighting in the trenches during World War I.

Who is the **audience** for this letter? What is the **register**? How does he show his passion for what he believes in?

P – You need to understand what a letter is and know your audience. **Register** is absolutely crucial with a letter. If you are applying for a job, for example, you need to keep the register formal.

C – It is important to tie your answer together using links and make sure you frequently refer back to the reason for writing the letter.

Exploring an open letter

Writing a formal letter is nothing new to you. The key thing to remember with an **open letter** is that your intended audience is everyone – not just one person.

In groups, look at the following sample paragraph for a 2019 exam paper question which asks you to respond to the view that young people today are a 'vain and selfish generation', and answer the questions.

Remember

Remember IRE: As you read the sample paragraph, put an '**I**' beside the **idea** that is stated, an '**R**' beside the **reference** to back up the idea, and an '**E**' beside the **explanation**.

Another label placed on young people today is that we are selfish. The writer says that all we are interested in is ourselves, and society has suffered because of it. But this is complete nonsense. Every day, teenagers all over Ireland are involved in charities and volunteering. The Scouts, football clubs, dance troupes – I could go on. We do it because we love to do it, and because we care about the community around us. This is not selfishness; it's pride in our area.

(84 words)

1. What claim has the writer argued against?

   _____

   _____

2. What rebuttal do they give?

   _____

   _____

Definition

Rebuttal: means you prove an argument against you is wrong.

How do we know that the writer of the original letter is not the only **audience** to this reply? Underline or highlight the evidence that shows this.

Question analysis

Look at the following question from the 2019 exam paper. Read it carefully before analysing it.

> Newspaper can be a print or online edition.

Question B – 50 marks

Your local newspaper has published a letter condemning 15 to 30-year-olds as a 'vain and selfish generation'. The letter-writer specifically refers to selfies as an example of the vanity of people in these age groups. Write **a letter to the newspaper editor**, in which you respond to the view expressed in the original letter, and put forward your own views on the subject of selfies.

> The editor is the person who runs the newspaper.

1. Who is the **audience** for a letter like this? _____

2. What **register** should you use when writing an **open letter** to a national newspaper like the *Irish Independent* or the *Irish Times*? _____

3. Put a number beside the things you are being asked to do in the last sentence.

4. Can you both agree *and* disagree with the statement? _____

Now we need to look at **structure** and **planning**. You will need to think about your answer before you start writing. You must include:

Structure – Letter to Editor

An introduction

- For **formal letters**, you will need to include your address and date in the top right and the receiver's address below it on the left. For an **open letter** you only need the date.

The Editor The Irish Times 24–28 Tara Street Dublin 2	20 February 2021 12 Chaseville Road Blanchardstown Dublin 15

Write 'Dear' and **the person's name**, if you know it. If you don't know their name, use their **job title**; for example, in this case, it would be 'Dear Editor'. Some people write 'Dear Sir/Dear Madam' if they don't know the name of the person they are writing to, but this can be considered old-fashioned.

- Set out clearly who you are and why you are writing. Always say what inspired you to write the letter.

- Plan out your answer and list the points you will be making.

The main body of the answer

- **Seven to eight** planned IRE paragraphs of about 70 words each.

- In an **open letter**, use rebuttal to show how the opposition is wrong and prove how you are right.

A conclusion

- Recap the points that you have made.

- Give your **contact details**, such as an email address or phone number.

- Leave the reader with something to think about, like a fact or a statement.

- Sign off formally with '**Yours sincerely**,' whether you know the person you're writing to or are using their job title.

- Then put down **your name** (signed and printed).

Overthinking

Sometimes in an exam, students can get bogged down overthinking small things that aren't important. For instance, in a letter the addresses need to be there, but they are not given in the question. So what do you do? Many students panic and spend ages trying to think of a made-up address for both themselves and the person or organisation they are writing to.

Simply have an address that you always use for these occasions. 123 Green Street, Trim, Co. Meath. Or 123 O'Connell Street, Dublin 1. The address is not that important, the answer is. So, get to *that* as quickly as possible and don't overthink the small things.

So, for the question we looked at earlier, we can now plan out what the **main body** will look like. There are **two** things that you are being asked to do, so you need to **plan them separately**. Make sure to mention **selfies** in some of your points as it tells you in the question that you have to mention them.

Are 15 to 30-year-olds 'vain and selfish'? Yes/No/A bit of both? _____

Why do you think this?

1. *NO – Young people get involved in volunteering.*
   YES – Always taking selfies and being on Instagram.

2. _____

3. _____

4. _____

What is your opinion of your generation?

1. *We have a lot of potential, but face struggles with money and jobs.*

2. _____

3. _____

4. _____

 Time to Write

Once you have finished your planning, you can now start working on writing your answer. As it is an **open letter**, remember that the audience is not just one person, but a whole group. Keep this in mind as you write your **introduction**.

A letter to the editor is an open letter. It will be about a specific topic but is designed to be read by everyone.

Comprehending B

Dear Editor,

3 December 2020

I am Elaine Caulfield, a young person and a regular reader of the Irish Times. In last week's edition I read _____

_____

_____

_____

> **Refer** to the question and use the question **keywords**.

I feel that this take on my generation is _____

_____

_____

> Give your **opinion** on the statement in the question. Do you agree or disagree with it? Or are you somewhere in the middle?

To prove this, and accurately represent my generation, I want to say _____

_____

_____

_____

> Write down **two to three** things that you will talk about.

> You were asked for your **opinion** on your generation, so what do you think young people are really like?

The **main body** paragraphs follow the same structure as the sample given earlier. Remember to use the **IRE** approach and to **link** your ideas.

In my view, young people today have a lot of potential but face many challenges. We have to _____

_____

This can be seen best when _____

_____

_____

> Give an **example** of when young people act like this.

_____

What we can see about my generation here is _____

_____

_____

> What does this **example show** about your generation? What kind of challenges do they overcome? What does it say about them as people? Are they hardworking? Lazy? Explain your point.

In the **conclusion**, remember that you have to speak to all of the people who will read this. This includes the people that agree with you *and* the people who agreed with the original letter. Try to convince them that your ideas about your generation are right.

A stereotypical image of what young people today, Generation Z, are like. Do you agree with it?

Now recap one or two of **your own ideas**.

In conclusion, many people reading this letter today might think _____

_____

For me, I feel that my generation is more like _____

_____

_____

_____

This is why I want to leave you with this: _____

_____

_____

_____

Yours sincerely,

Finally, think of something to leave the reader with. Think of a statement that begins something like: 'The next time you want to say something about young people, try to consider …'

Elaine Caulfield
_____
ELAINE CAULFIELD

Time to Finish

With your answer planned and some sample paragraphs done, it's now time to complete your answer on a separate page.

Time to Impress

Address the other side

One important way of making your own point stronger is to have a look at what the argument against you is, and then prove it wrong. It makes your argument weaker if you never address the point that is made against you in the first place.

> Give a made-up example of someone who might fit this description.

The author may have a point when they call us 'vain'. We all know _____

_____

_____

However, to call all of us that is just plain wrong as _____

_____

> Prove them wrong by showing how most young people are different.

Class/Homework exercise

- Read and analyse the following questions.
- Then plan out your answers.
- Finally, write full 50-mark answers.

1. Kailash Satyarthi is a human rights activist from India who has been a leader in the global movement to end child slavery. Based on what you have read about him, you have decided to write **a letter to the editor of a national newspaper**. You want to encourage people to become more aware of the problem of children working in poor conditions in developing countries. In your letter you should give some information about this problem and express your strong views on the subject. (2018)

2. Imagine it is proposed that all the teachers in Irish schools will be replaced by robots. Write **a letter to the editor of a national newspaper** giving reasons why you do or do not support the proposed change from human to robot teachers. (2017)

3. Imagine NASA has advertised looking for a young person to be part of their next moon mission. Write **a letter of application**, emphasising your suitability for a position on the team. (2011)

 ## Time to Reflect

1. How is the audience for an **open letter/letter to the editor** different to a formal letter?

2. How is the **register** affected by this?

3. Why do you think **open letters** are written? Why not address it only to the person it's intended for?

4. Who is the **audience** for the following kinds of letters: invitation, job application, editor of a newspaper, competition entry?

5. You should always finish your letter with a **statement** or a **question**. What does this add to your writing?

LESSON 19: COMPREHENDING A – AUTOBIOGRAPHY – *RECOVERING* BY RICHIE SADLIER

Learning Objectives – By the end of this lesson you should:

- Know what an **autobiography** is and how it's different to a biography
- Be able to **analyse the questions** and the **autobiography extract** shown
- Be able to **plan** and **write** coherent answers

 Time to Think

In an **autobiography**, an individual looks back on their life and writes about it. Because it's the author's own view, it gives the reader a real **personal insight**. However, an **autobiography** is naturally one-sided (biased). The author may leave out controversial things or just tell outright lies. Why might they do this? A **biography** is when someone else tells the person's story. How is a **biography** more likely to be balanced?

Have you ever read someone's **autobiography**? Whose was it? Do you think that they were always truthful?

If you were to write your own autobiography, what events would you put in? What would you leave out? Why?

Similar to the **novel excerpt**, in the exam you will only be given a small section of text that could be from anywhere in the autobiography, so make sure to read the **context** carefully.

Before you read …

How important is support from your parents/guardians when it comes to achieving your goals?

How do you overcome setbacks in your life?

Question analysis

Read and plan your answers using **CARPA** (Context, Analyse, Read, Plan, Answer). Refer back to **Lesson 3** (pages 15–16) if you need more detail on each step.

TRYING TO BECOME A PROFESSIONAL FOOTBALLER

> **Read the context to the question.**

The following is an edited extract from the award-winning autobiography *Recovering* by former Irish soccer international, now RTÉ pundit, Richie Sadlier. In his memoir, Richie recounts how he achieved his goal of becoming a professional footballer and his struggle with mental health issues when he had to retire early due to injury. It also deals with his alcoholism and sexual abuse he suffered as a teenager. This extract deals with parental support and Richie's first trials with English football clubs.

1. When I was sixteen, my dad started to regularly watch me play at Belvedere. Nobody said anything. I didn't know what had changed, and he only ever came if Mum was coming too, but I noticed. Of course I noticed.

2. I was playing the best football I'd ever produced at the highest level I'd ever played, and now, each time I looked to the side-lines, Dad was there. He never once criticised my performances or grilled me about anything. There were no post-game dressing-downs that other lads got from their dads, no input from the touchline that overstepped the mark. He just asked if I was happy with how I had played, and he left it at that. I never once told him how much it meant to me that he was there.

3. If I craved Dad's approval, it was Mum who kept things going. I would talk to her about everything, and if I needed something, she would find a way of getting it for me. As football became more serious, she managed to scrape together £65 for a new pair of Mizuno boots, which was a lot back in 1994 and a far cry from the £2 boots I wore when I started out. There was one condition: I couldn't tell anyone she'd paid for them. When Belvedere were playing in a summer tournament in Wales, it was Mum who found the money, and it was handed over again on the basis that nobody ever know it came from her. After I signed my first professional contract, one of the first things I did was pay my mum back the money she had spent to help me get there. I kept a record of all she'd paid for and when she came to visit, I gave her a cheque for £800. I owed her a lot more than money, though.

4. The possibility of moving abroad was also starting to emerge. Before Belvedere, I had never spoken to anyone who had been on trial with an English club, but now I had teammates who could tell me what was involved. And my Belvedere managers, Gerry, Peadar Behan and Vincent Butler, were telling me I should set that as my main target. This was different from being encouraged by Mum or any of my teachers in St Benildus College. This was praise from people who knew what it took to play at that level.

5. One night, in February 1995, Gerry Smullen, the Millwall scout in Ireland called to our house to invite me over on trial. It was barely six months since I had joined Belvedere. Mum and Dad were with me when he outlined what would be involved. I can still remember the buzz in the room that night. None of us really knew how to react, other than to just say, 'Yes'.

6. Millwall weren't the only club showing an interest. I went on trial to Bolton Wanderers when I was sixteen, but I totally froze. Unsurprisingly, I wasn't asked back. But once I went to Millwall, my mind was made up. Millwall, it's fair to say, probably took a bit longer to make their mind up about me. I first went over there for a week at Easter when I was in fifth year. I told the lads on the team my name but maybe they didn't catch it, they seemed happy to call me Paddy. I wasn't pleased about that, but I was sixteen and there were a lot of them.

7. On the field, with so much at stake, I froze again. In a practise game against Watford, everyone was bigger, faster and stronger. I felt completely out of my depth. I have the generosity of Millwall's youth development officer to thank for not calling a halt to everything there and then. He must have realised that what I produced couldn't have been my normal level or I wouldn't have got that far. Millwall offered me a two-year deal that summer after seeing me play for Belvedere in the tournament in Wales. Signing would have meant not sitting my Leaving Cert. Amazingly, and for that reason, I turned it down.

8. Over fifty players had moved to the UK from Belvedere by that time and only two went on to have careers in the game. Despite obsessing about an offer like this for as long as I could remember, I said no because I felt I needed a plan B. Maybe part of me just wasn't ready to take the plunge.

Read and analyse text and images.

IMAGE 19:2

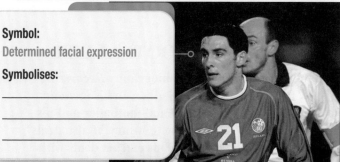

IMAGE 19:1

RICHIE SADLIER
Recovering

Symbol:
Determined facial expression

Symbolises:
_____
_____
_____

Symbol:
Irish jersey

Symbolises:
Playing for your country. The best moment of a player's career.

Symbol:
Looking straight at the camera

Symbolises:
_____
_____
_____

Symbol:
Dark cover with plain letters

Symbolises:
_____
_____
_____

Question A – 50 marks

(i) From your reading of the autobiography extract, outline the support Richie Sadlier received in his quest to become a professional footballer. Support your answer with reference to the text. (15)

1. _____

2. _____

3. _____

Read and analyse the questions.

(ii) From your reading of the extract, which of the following words or phrases do you think best describes Richie Sadlier at this time in his life? 1: Talented. 2: Lacking confidence. 3: Levelheaded. (15)

1. _____

2. _____

3. _____

(iii) (a) IMAGE 19:1 shows Richie Sadlier making his debut for Ireland against Russia in 2002. Imagine you are Richie Sadlier at the press conference after the game. You are asked the question 'How do you feel about making your debut?' Write your response. (10)

1. _____

2. _____

Plan your answers.

(b) IMAGE 19:2 shows the cover of Richie Sadlier's autobiography. Does it make you want to read the book? Why? (10)

1. _____

2. _____

Answer the question using IRE.

Comprehending A

Tip For Success

Outline

A question beginning with '**outline**' can often confuse students. 'Outline' just means to give a **brief description**. It doesn't mean that you have to give your own opinion.

The key to getting a better mark in these questions is to **explain your point**. Give a **brief explanation** and then add some **analysis**. When the question asks you to **outline** the support Richie Sadlier received, writing 'his mum bought his boots' isn't enough. **Outline how hard** it was for her to come up with the money. **Outline how thankful** he was. Always add in a bit of **depth** to an **outline** question.

LESSON 20: COMPREHENDING B – COMPETITION ENTRIES

Learning Objectives – By the end of this lesson you should:

- Know what a **competition entry** is and how it is different from a **formal letter**
- Know the **audience** and **register** for a **competition entry**
- Be able to **plan** and **write** a 500-word answer for a Comprehending B question

 Time to Think

Sometimes, to win a competition you have to write an entry where you are asked to set out, clearly and in a detailed way, *why* you should win. You could be asked to describe why you deserve a place on a course, why your town should win a local award, or why your club should be given a grant to buy new equipment. Your entry will be read by a judge; so how are you going to convince them to choose your entry over everyone else's?

Do you ever enter competitions?

Have you ever won a competition? What did you have to do to win?

Here is an example of a writing competition for women writers from a group called WOW! Women on Writing. Read below what they are looking for in their entries for their flash fiction competition:

> Seeking short fiction of any genre between 250–750 words. The mission of this contest is to inspire creativity, communication, and give well-rewarded recognition to contestants. Upon the close of our contest, and after the winners have been announced, you will receive a critique from one of our judges on three categories:
>
> Subject [what the story was about].
>
> Content [what was in the story].
>
> Technical [how the story was written].
>
> You will be provided with your scores (1 to 5) in each category.

This is the logo for Women on Writing's Flash Fiction competition. Do you think it is effective?

Definition

> **Flash fiction**: a really short story, only a few paragraphs long.

Definition

> **Criteria**: means the things you will be judged on in the competition. They are usually listed in the question.

What **word limit** is given to the person looking to enter? What **three things** are the judges looking at? As you can see, every competition has a set of **criteria** that the competition judges will look at, so it's vital to remember to keep them in mind when you write your **competition entry**.

PCLM

> **P** – Make sure you understand that you have to **convince** the competition judges that your entry deserves to win over all other entries.
>
> **L** – The languages of **persuasion**, **argument**, and **information** are key here.

Exploring a competition entry

Using the language of **persuasion** is vital for a **competition entry**.

In groups, look at the following sample answer to a 2016 exam question that asked Leaving Certificate students to say why they deserved a free holiday:

Remember

Remember IRE: As you read the sample paragraph, put an 'I' beside the **idea** that is stated, an 'R' beside the **reference** to back up the idea, and an 'E' beside the **explanation**.

I understand that there will be many people who feel they should win this massive prize, but I think that I should get it because of how hard I've had to work to get this far. I have had to get a part-time job, as well as study, because the course I want to do next year is so expensive. This means that I've had very little time to myself and a holiday is just what I need after this tough year.

(82 words)

1. What **idea** does the writer give as to why they should win the prize?

   _____

   _____

2. Why do you think the writer refers to the other people who have entered the competition?

   _____

   _____

3. How does the writer **link** their point back to the question?

   _____

   _____

Question analysis

Now that we know what a **competition entry** should read like, it is time to fully analyse a past exam question.

> **Question B – 50 marks**
>
> A travel company is running a competition for Leaving Certificate students. The prize is a post-examination holiday to a destination chosen by the winner. Entrants are required to outline where they would go, give reasons why they would like to travel there, and explain why they deserve to win the holiday. Write the **competition entry** you would submit. (2016)

1. Who is running the competition? _____

2. Who will be judging the competition? _____

3. What do you think they are looking for in the winning entry?

   _____

4. Reread the third sentence, the one beginning with 'Entrants are…' Mark the number of parts in the question.

Structure – Competition Entry

An introduction

- Write 'Dear _____,' with **the name of the person** running the competition and the date. If you're not sure, use their **job title** or the name of the company; for example, 'Dear Competition Judge' or 'Dear WinLoads & Co'.

- Set out clearly **who you are** and **why you are writing**.

- **Plan out** your answer and list the points you feel should allow you to win the prize.

The main body of the answer

- **Seven to eight planned IRE paragraphs** of about 70 words each.

- Be **convincing** and make sure to **refer to the prize and criteria** throughout.

A conclusion

- **Recap** the points that you made.

- Give your **contact details** (a made-up email or phone number).

- Finish by reminding the judges how you **deserve** the prize.

- **Sign off** by writing, 'Yours sincerely,' and then signing and printing your name.

The question has **three** parts to it. So now it's time to plan them out.

Where do you want to go? _____

A. Describe the place as best you can.

1. *It's a beautiful place with golden sands and warm waters*

   or

2. *It's an exciting place with biking trails and kayaking on the lake.*

3. _____
   _____

4. _____
   _____

How does this image of a bike trail convey excitement?

B. Why do you want to go here?

1. *It's a place I've always dreamed of visiting, ever since I saw a picture of it on TV when I was young.*

2. _____
   _____

3. _____
   _____

C. Why do you deserve the prize?

1. I've had to work really hard during my Leaving Cert year, and I've even had to take a part-time job. I really need a rest.

2. _____
   _____

3. _____
   _____

How does this image of a tranquil beach convey relaxation?

✍ Time to Write

Now that the planning is completed, it's time to move on to writing the answer.

Firstly, you need an **introduction**. Focus on setting out who you are and the reasons why your entry deserves to be the winning entry.

> Give your reason for writing. Use the **key question** words.

Dear Competition Judge,   14 October 2021

I am Tomás Ó Sé, and I am writing this letter to _____
_____

I feel that I should win the marvellous prize on offer because _____
_____
_____
_____

> Write two of your reasons here to show you have a **plan**.

The **main body** paragraphs follow the same structure as the sample answer given earlier. Remember to use the **IRE** approach and to **link** your ideas. In this example you would give the reasons why you would like to travel to this place.

> When did you see this place for the first time? Where were you? How old were you? Was it in a magazine or on TV?

This place has always meant so much to me. The first time I ever saw it was _____
_____
_____

I just loved the _____
_____
_____

> What about the place made you love it? The people? The views? Describe why.

Why does all of this make you want to visit the place?

Since that moment, I have wanted to _____
_____
_____
_____

Finally, you will need to write a **conclusion**. This will be the last thing the judge will read before they decide if you deserve the prize or not, so make sure it is **convincing**.

So, to sum up, going here would be an amazing experience for me.

Recap two to three of your points.

I think I am deserving of the prize because _____
_____
_____
_____

You can contact me at any time on/at _____
_____

Give your contact details.

To win this prize would be a dream come true, and I hope that _____

Finish by saying how much you want the prize.

_____
_____

Tomás Ó Sé
_____

TOMÁS Ó SÉ

Time to Finish

With your answer planned and some sample paragraphs done, it's now time to complete your answer on a separate page.

Simon Cowell is a judge on Britain's Got Talent. *Contestants need to impress him and the other judges when they audition.*

 **Time to Impress**

Talk to the judges

Imagine you were one of the judges in a competition like this. You would have to read through hundreds, if not thousands, of entries. What would make one stand out over the other? One way is for the writer of the entry to call up this fact:

I know that you have to read so many deserving entries, but I really feel that mine stands out because of how hard I've worked over the last two years.

Finish the next two yourself:

I can only imagine the difficulty of having to go through hundreds of entries; however _____

_____

_____

_____

_____

I'm sure you have piles of letters in front of you, but I hope mine touches your heart because

_____

_____

_____

_____

_____

Comprehending B

Tip For Success

Idioms

We use **idioms** all the time, even if we don't recognise the name. If you are 'over the moon' at some news, then you aren't literally in space. You are just happy. What about being 'cash-strapped'? Is cash strapped to you or are you short of a few euro? Idioms make your work more interesting and will increase your **language** mark. Make sure to only use them if the tone is semi-formal or informal. So, try use some of the following in your writing:

- Spill the beans – let out a secret.
- Let your hair down – relax.
- Touch your heart – feel emotional about something.
- A bitter pill to swallow – doing something you don't want to do but have to.
- Not rocket science – when you think something is easy to do or understand.
- Use your head – think about it.

There are thousands more, so look some of them up to use in your future answers.

Class/Homework exercise

- Read and analyse the following questions.
- Then plan out your answers.
- Finally, write full 50-mark answers.

1. The Irish Film Association is looking for the next generation of directors, actors, producers, and stylists. They are running a competition for a paid internship for the summer in any of the four positions. Write your **competition entry** explaining your love of film, why you are perfect for the internship, and what you think you will get from doing it. (Sample)

2. Your local area wishes to enter the Best Community in the Country competition. You have been asked to create the **competition entry**. The entry must explain why you think your town has the best community and also what you intend to do with the €50,000 prize money if you win. (Sample)

3. Your school entered a competition where the winners would be given a free trip to a European city of their choice. But the school can only bring twenty students on the trip. Students who wish to go have to write a **competition entry**, to be judged by the principal, outlining where they would like to go and why they are deserving of a place on the journey. (Sample)

 Time to Reflect

1. What is the main purpose of a **competition entry**?
2. Are you the only person entering the competition? How does this affect your entry?
3. Why is it important to stick to the **criteria** you are given?
4. Should you **speak directly** to the judge? Why?

COMPOSING

About this section: Composing

Lessons 21–27 will help you develop skills that you can use in the Personal essay and the Short story Composition questions.

Planning work and sample answers on both types of writing are included in each of the lessons.

Lesson 28 and 29 will guide you in your planning of personal essays and short stories.

Lessons 30 and 31 will help you in answering speech and article questions that come up in the Composition section of the paper.

LESSON 21: POINTS OF VIEW

Learning Objectives – By the end of this lesson you should:

- Know the benefits of the using a **first person** and a **third person narrator**
- Know the drawbacks and limitations of using different **points of view**
- Be able to write a sample narrative in the **first person** and the **third person**

 ## Time to Think

A writer needs to think about who is narrating the story or essay they are creating. Is it the writer themselves? Then it is in the **first person**. This is the **only** kind of narrator for a **personal essay**, but you can also use it for a **short story**.

First person narration: When the writer uses 'I' and tells the story as if it happened to themselves.

Third person narration: When the writer uses 'he', 'she', 'it' or 'they', and tells the story as though it happened to someone else.

A **first person narrator** makes your work far more personal. The reader can really see it from **your point of view** and can **empathise** with you a lot more. Why is this a benefit to writing in the **first person**? But, a **first person narrator** doesn't know what is going on in other people's heads – what they are thinking; why they do what they do – unless the other person tells them or they see it happening. And even then, a **first person narrator** could be lying or faking (this is called an 'unreliable' narrator). Why does this make writing in the **first person** difficult? What drawbacks does it create?

Definition

Empathy: means when a reader understands why a character acted the way they did. They don't have to feel sorry for them, though.

Here is a famous example of a **first person narrator**: Red from *The Shawshank Redemption* – who is played by actor Morgan Freeman in the movie:

First person.

I came to Shawshank when I was just twenty, and I am one of the few people in our happy little family willing to own up to what they did. I committed murder. I put a large insurance policy on my wife, who was three years older than I was, and then I fixed the brakes of the Chevrolet coupe her father had given us as a wedding present. It worked out exactly as I had planned, except I hadn't planned on her stopping to pick up the neighbor woman and the neighbor woman's infant son on their way down Castle Hill and into town.

From *The Shawshank Redemption* by Stephen King

This is a scene from the movie adaptation of the Stephen King novella. Red, the narrator in the excerpt, is on the right.

Do you think the narrator is **reliable**? What does this mean about the rest of his story? Do you have any sympathy for him?

But you can also have a **third person narrator**. They can describe the action from the **perspective of any of the characters**. A key drawback comes from this freedom. Why do you think it can be a little harder to connect with a character's journey told from the **perspective** of a number of characters?

Here is a famous example of storytelling in the **third person**. It is from a text that is often on the Leaving Certificate course.

Third person.

When Jane and Elizabeth were alone, the former, who had been cautious in her praise of Mr Bingley before, expressed to her sister how very much she admired him.

'He is just what a young man ought to be,' said she, 'sensible, good humoured, lively; and I never saw such happy manners!'

From *Pride and Prejudice* by Jane Austen

Rosamund Pike as Jane Bennet, Keira Knightley as Elizabeth Bennet and Simon Woods as Charles Bingley in Pride and Prejudice.

Where was the **narrator** during the conversation? Could anyone see them? Why do we only get to know what Jane really thought of Mr Bingley after he left the room? Would she tell us what she thought of him sooner if it was in the **first person**? These are things you will need to consider as you write in the **third person**.

PCLM

P – Questions like the **personal essay**, the **article**, and the **speech** require you to write in the **first person** only. Know the strengths and drawbacks of this style. For a **short story**, you can have a **first person** or **third person** narrator.

L – Being able to express yourself in any **point of view** means focusing on **description** and **emotion**.

Exploring points of view

First person narrator

When you are writing from a **first person** perspective, you need to know what the style can do and what it can't. Look at the following sample paragraph from the 2017 **personal essay** exam question about the importance of praise and encouragement:

First person.

I always wanted my dad to praise me, but the words never really came. He would show up at my matches and just stand there, looking at his phone. Looking back, it would have been better if he hadn't ever been there at all. I felt so down, so discouraged. If only he had said a few words of inspiration, then it could have made such a difference. He never actually spoke a word. His face always told me he'd rather be somewhere else.

(84 words)

1. What did the narrator want to happen?

   _____

   _____

2. What did the father do instead?

   _____

   _____

3. How did the narrator feel?

   _____

   _____

4. How did the father feel about being there? What evidence is there? Does he speak?

   _____

   _____

Third person narrator

When writing in the **third person**, you get to decide how much freedom the narrator has. You can use **third person narration** to follow just one character's point of view. Or you can narrate the story using more than one character's point of view. Look at these two examples of **third person narration** and answer the questions on them. They both look at the same scene, but they show the two different styles of **third person narration** and different **points of view**.

The room was empty, cold, and dark. A single light flickered from a candle in the corner. Sam had lit it earlier, knowing that Eva would arrive at midnight. It was now 2 a.m. There was a squeak of a floorboard outside the room. Slowly, the door creaked open. The sound was made louder by the silence before it.

Third person.

Downstairs, Sam left the house by the back door. Eva was late, and he was fed up waiting. He angrily slammed the door shut as he left and walked across the grass.

Upstairs, creeping across the candlelit room, Eva jumped.

(99 words)

1. Circle the three words at the start that describe the room. What atmosphere does this create?

   _____

2. Look again at how Eva enters the room. What does this tell us about how she feels?

   _____

   _____

3. What new location does the paragraph move to? _____

4. Why is it helpful for the narrator to be able to move from place to place? What are the drawbacks of doing that?

   _____

   _____

Tip For Success

Switching point of view

When writing **more than one point of view in third person narration**, make sure you don't jump constantly from one character to the next, as your reader will find the story difficult to follow. Make it clear each time **which character's perspective** you are **focusing** on. How do you think this is done in the sample paragraphs above?

Composing

Here is the same scene again, except this time the narrator **only follows Eva's point of view**. Look at the way **tension** is built up in the paragraph:

Why is it important to create atmosphere when you are writing a scene?

Third person. Eva knew she was late – way late – but she moved cautiously through the cold, dark house. Ever since she was a kid the ruin always freaked her out. But she had made a promise to Sam. And even though it took far longer to sneak out of her house than she thought it would, she was going to keep that promise. She gently pushed the door to the room open. She knew it was the right one as she could see the candle flicker through the keyhole. The door screeched loudly in the dead of night. The room was empty. All of sudden, a door downstairs slammed. Her blood ran cold.

(111 words)

1. Why was Eva late? Did we know this in the other example? _____

2. How does she feel about the abandoned house?

   _____

   _____

3. When Sam slammed the door at the end, does Eva know it was him? _____

4. Because you are only following Eva, how might this create **tension**?

   _____

   _____

Tip For Success

Other people's perspective

Writing from **another person's perspective** can be tough. We looked at this back in **Lesson 8** on diary entries: 'Imagine you are …' But sometimes in a short story, you have no choice but to pretend you are someone else entirely. In 2018, there was an exam question about identical twins and another about preventing a disaster. What if you're an only child who has never been in a disaster? In 2017, there was even a question about a being a robot teacher!

Make sure to spend a few minutes planning the kind of person you are being asked to imagine. If you have to create them from scratch, make them **believable** and **well-rounded**. Give them a **past** and a **personality** so that the reader can **empathise** with them.

Question analysis

Look at the following questions and try to think about the kind of **first person narrator** you could have:

1. Write a **personal essay** in which you discuss what you think your life would be like if you were unable to use any form of social media for a whole year. (2019)

I am a regular Sixth Year student who uses social media a lot. I'm very outgoing and rely on tech to keep in touch. It would be a huge change to my life to give it up.

2. Write a **short story** which features two characters who hold opposing points of view. (2016)

I am running for president, but I am also very corrupt. What I want to do as president is _____

_____

_____

_____

> What do you want to do when you are president?

My challenger is clean and _____

_____

_____

_____

> What does your challenger promise to do? Why is it important that the reader knows they are different?

Now try to think of a **third person narrator**:

3. Write a **short story** which features a character who gets into trouble because of their sense of humour. (2017)

Saheed [the third person narrator] works backstage in a comedy club. As he moves about, he can hear the performers talking in their dressing rooms, and the audience as they talk to each other in their seats. One night, the big act, Alice Stone, tells a joke she shouldn't have and Saheed follows the fallout.

4. Write a **short story** where the main character goes on an exciting journey and learns some valuable lessons along the way. (2016)

Anna is a bit quiet and doesn't really have that much confidence in herself. But one day she decides to go on a solo trip around the world. _____

_____

_____

> Where does Anna go? What happens while she's there? What does she learn about herself?

5. Write a **short story** in which a group of childhood friends form what becomes a world-famous band but live to regret their success. (2019)

_____

_____

_____

 **Time to Write**

First person narrator

Now we are going to look at both styles of **first person** writing: the **personal essay** and the **short story**, using two of the sample questions above.

Personal essay on 'social media'

> First person.

> What do you do on social media?

I am a bit of an addict when it comes to social media. Every day _____
_____

> How does it make you feel when you use it? Think of the positives and the negatives.

It makes me feel _____
_____
_____
_____

> What looks does your mam give you? Is she happy at the amount of time you spend on social media? Think of her eyes, her mouth, her body language.

But it just takes one look at my mam's face to tell me _____
_____
_____

As you can see, you really only know what is going on in your (the narrator's) head. You can only guess at what other people think. This applies to the first person narrator in a **short story** composition question from the 2019 exam paper (see 5. on page 109):

We can learn a lot about how a person thinks by simply looking at them. Sometimes it tells us more than words can.

Short story on the 'world-famous band'

> First person.

> Describe what you saw. Did the others look happy? Sad? Frustrated? How could you tell?

I looked at the rest of them in the studio that day. They all seemed _____
_____

> How did this make you feel? Did it make you want to get out of there? Why?

This all made me feel _____
_____
_____

> What about the way Tamara looked told you how she was thinking? Her eyes? Her mouth? Her body language? Don't focus only on what she might say.

I knew Tamara could read my mind. She didn't speak, but the look on her face said _____
_____
_____

Third person narrator

Next, we will look at **short story** writing from the **point of view** of a **third person narrator** with the 2017 paper sense of humour question (3 on page 109).

Third person.

Alice crept through the open doors of the club and headed for her dressing room. She glanced at _____

_____

What did Alice Stone see as she looked around the club?

What couldn't she do? Why was she worried? Why not just tell the joke anyway?

She was worried. She saw Tommy Sheehan sitting there – the head of the local mob. She couldn't possibly _____

_____

What was going through her head as she sat in the dressing room? What options did she have?

But she also knew it was her best joke in the routine. She was conflicted as she sat in her dressing room over whether _____

_____

 Time to Impress

Behind those eyes …

When you are writing in the **first person**, a major difficulty is that you can't fully know what is going on in someone else's head. Even if they speak, the words may not be the truth. Think about the amount of times a friend said they were fine; but were they? Here we are going to work on using this in a story or an essay. Read the example below and finish off the samples that follow it.

All samples are in the first person.

Seán looked right at me and said, 'Don't worry. It wasn't your fault.' But behind those eyes, I could tell that he was lying. They were cold and brutal. He still blamed me for what happened, and, to be honest, he was probably right.

Orla went to say something to me and then stopped. The strain of it seemed to be killing her. There was a dark fire in her eyes I'd never seen before. She desperately wanted to tell me

_____

Caelum raised his voice and said, 'I'll do it.' The words were clear, but the troubled look in his eyes told me something else. _____

_____

_____

Susannah was playing it cool. 'Sure, I suppose I could go,' she said, as calm as you like. But I could see the fear in her eyes, although she did her best to hide it.

_____

The **third person narrator** gives you the freedom to go anywhere and show two different perspectives at once. This can show the confusion the characters are feeling. It can also create **tension** in a scene.

> **All the samples are in the third person.**

Maya sat on the park bench, waiting. The hour had come and gone, and yet Michael had still not appeared. She thought she had been stood up and tears welled in her eyes. What she didn't know was that Michael was stuck in detention. He stared at the clock in desperation. He knew Maya would never forgive him.

The garda jumped out of the car and grabbed Craig, who fit the description that was given over the radio. Little did Craig know _____

> **Was it a case of mistaken identity? Was Craig being set up? How did Craig react?**

_____

Enda got down on one knee in the crowded restaurant. He knew he loved Louise with all his heart. What he couldn't know was _____

> **What did Enda not know? What was she keeping from him?**

_____

Class/Homework exercise

- Read the following scenes.
- Brainstorm descriptions and emotions that could be present in the scene. An example is given for the first question.
- Finally, write a **first person narrator** paragraph describing what happens. Make sure to keep it in the past tense.

1. Brenda is talking about school. She is popular and outgoing, but also wants to do well in class. She talks about the time her friends invited her out the night before a big test.

   Brainstorming: Worried she might fail the test. Afraid of what her friends might think of her if she doesn't go. Knows she shouldn't care but does. Sees the look in her friends' faces as they ask. Knows how they will look at her if she bails.

2. Alexei's father wants him to get involved in the family business when he finishes school, but he wants to go to college to do Sports Science. He talks about this when he sits his father down to tell him his decision.

- **Brainstorm** the next two scenes.
- Then write a **third person narrator** paragraph describing what happens. Remember to look at the scene from different viewpoints. Make sure to keep it in the **past** tense.

1. The Year Head, Mr Meagher, is doing spot checks on lockers because he has received a tip-off that someone has something they shouldn't have in one of them.

2. A politician is being offered a bribe from an undercover reporter. The scene takes place in a crowded bar.

 **Time to Reflect**

1. What benefits are there to writing in the **first person**?

2. What benefits are there to writing in the **third person**?

3. What drawbacks are there to using either kind of narrator?

4. Why is body language and facial expression so important in a **first person** essay or story?

5. How honest is the narrator themselves? Can you always **trust** them?

6. Why must you make sure you don't switch between **first person** and **third person** narrator in your work?

LESSON 22: THEME

Learning Objectives – By the end of this lesson you should:

- Know how to find the **theme** in a question
- Be able to **explore** a theme before writing
- Be able to write a **theme** section using two different styles: (a) *Everyone and then me* and (b) *Description and reveal*

 ## Time to Think

Before a writer begins a piece of writing, they will always consider what the central point of the essay or story will be. If the plot has two kids growing up together, then the **theme** could be friendship. If it's about someone recovering from an injury to perform in the big final, then the **theme** could be **overcoming obstacles**.

Think about *Game of Thrones* or any other famous books or television shows. What are the **themes** in the story? What were the writers trying to get the viewer to think about?

Here's a famous opening paragraph where the **theme** of mystery and magic is explored from the very start:

> Mr and Mrs Dursley, of number four, Privet Drive, were proud to say that they were perfectly normal, thank you very much. They were the last people you'd expect to be involved in anything strange or mysterious, because they just didn't hold with such nonsense.

From *Harry Potter and the Philosopher's Stone* by J.K. Rowling

How does the **theme** jump out at the reader? What words are used that explore this **theme**? What is the attitude of the Dursleys to the **theme**? Straight away we get an impression of what the story will be about. Whatever the **theme**, it is important for the writer to know what it is and explore it before they begin their story.

The famous cover from the book that began the Harry Potter series. Can you see how the theme of magic is shown in the illustration?

PCLM

P – You are showing the examiner that you really understand the question and that you have not missed the **key question word**, in this case, the **theme**.

C – A strong **introduction** sets the **tone** for a **coherent** story. It shows **planning and foresight**, so keep this in mind.

L – This is an opportunity to use **aesthetic** language. Try to set yourself apart from the rest sitting the exam by being as **descriptive** and **original** as possible.

Working the theme into your answer

It is important that you talk about the **theme** in the question throughout your answer. It isn't enough to mention it at the start, and then feel that you've done enough. To maximise your **purpose** mark, you have to work it into your answer throughout.

A good way of doing this is through **synonyms**. For example, if the theme is 'praise' like in the 2017 paper, then you could use words and phrases like 'approval' and 'positive words'. Also talk about the impact of the theme: '**I was delighted to hear her say that...**' Just make sure you mention it throughout your answer a number of times, as it helps show the examiner that you have stayed on track.

Definition

Synonyms: means words that mean the same thing or something similar to another word.

Exploring theme

Being able to write about **theme** really sets a piece of writing apart from the rest. Think of the examiner getting to a paper that is midway through their bundle that opens like this:

The way your best friend is always supposed to be there for you is the thing that gets me the most. When you're down, they are by your side, picking you back up. When you receive the best news ever, they are cheering you along with a pride only a best friend can show. But what happens when this is put in danger? What was I supposed to do after making that one huge mistake?

(75 words)

1. In pairs, decide what **themes** the writer may have had in mind and list them.

   _____

   _____

2. What do you think sets this opening apart from the many other the examiner has to correct?

   _____

   _____

   _____

Question analysis

After analysing a paragraph on **theme**, we can now look at the following sample essay titles and circle what you think the **themes** are (there can be more than one theme in a question text). The first one is circled for you.

1. Write a short story where the main character undergoes a (transformation.) (Sample)

2. Write a short story about a character whose determination to be the centre of attention has unexpected consequences. (2019)

3. Write a personal essay in which you discuss what you have already achieved in life and what you hope to achieve in the future. (2018)

4. Write a short story which involves a race against time to prevent a disaster. (2018)

5. Write a personal essay giving your views on the importance of praise and encouragement as we go through life. (2017)

Once you know the **theme** for your short story or personal essay, you can brainstorm what it means to you and to others. After this is done, you can include some of these ideas in your answer. This also shows the examiner that you really know what the question is about, enhancing your **purpose** mark.

Composing

In this example, a writer has **brainstormed** the **theme** of **transformation**:

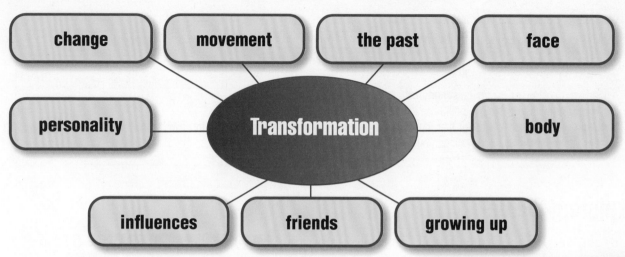

At first the ideas are straightforward – 'change' is just a **synonym** for 'transformation'. Then, there are **transformations** you can see, like 'face' and 'body'. But as you look a little deeper at the **theme**, you can see other themes like 'growing up' and 'friends'. How can we see **transformation** in these themes?

Now let's look at the **theme** of **difficulty**.

1. List some synonyms for 'difficulty'. Then think of words that mean the *opposite*, and write those down too.

    _____

    _____

The theme of transformation offers the writer a chance to discuss change and how it can be an opportunity for positive development.

2. What causes difficulty in your life?

    _____

    _____

3. What/who helps you overcome difficulties?

    _____

    _____

Now **brainstorm** the **theme** of **growing up** from the 2018 paper.

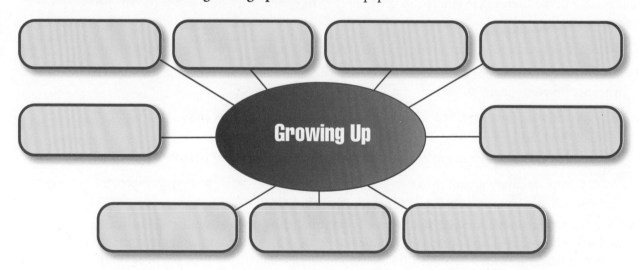

Pair/Group work ideas:

Do out a **brainstorm** diagram for each of the following **themes** using the skills you worked on earlier:

- Childhood (2019)
- Family (2018)
- Friends (2018)
- Regret (2017)
- Journeys (2016)

 ## Time to Write

Now you can begin writing your opening paragraph. This beginning works for both the **short story** and the **personal essay**. The most obvious way is to explain what it means to you. Unfortunately, this often comes out like a shopping list and not a story.

> Growing up is a time in our lives when we are young. We grow up right from when we are kids. There are different stages to growing up. We are babies, then we are toddlers, then we go to school ...

This won't be very interesting for your reader. Let's look at two techniques to talk about **theme** in a more interesting and creative way.

Everyone and then me

For this technique, you need to think of the **theme** in terms of:

- How it affects everyone.
- And how it affects you (or the character in the story).

> We all grow up. Whether you're born into a tribal village in Kenya or a rural town in Galway, we all experience this period of our lives that shapes us into the adults we will become. We fight with our brothers and sisters; we play with our friends in the grass. For most, it is a time of joy and wonder, of magic and self-discovery. For me, it was a time of danger and difficulty, of self-doubt and recovery.
>
> (79 words)

An English basket weaver meeting with Kenyan weavers. Even though they are continents apart, they grew up learning the same skills.

1. First off, list the examples that happen to everyone:

   _____

   _____

   _____

Composing

2. But how was the character's experience of growing up different?

_____

_____

Now that we've looked at an example, let's practise with the **theme** of **school** (2018).

First off, write down **two** things that you think everyone experiences in school:

1. _____

2. _____

For a **personal essay**, think about how these things had an impact on **you**.

Now imagine you are inventing a character for a story based on the theme of **school**. This character needs to stand out, so list two ways in which your character's experience of school could be different to everyone else's:

1. _____

2. _____

Once you've explored the impact and have thought of the differences, you can write a paragraph of real quality on the **theme** of **school**. The key is to make the character – whether it's you or a made-up person – **compelling**. This is why we will care about them when something bad happens to them later in the story.

School was always a busy and demanding place. Every day you'd see _____

_____

But for me, it was different. _____

_____

> **Describe school life for everyone else.**

> **Now say how life was different for you. Be descriptive and use emotion in your writing.**

Description and reveal

This technique is another way to explore a **theme** deeply. It shows real creativity as, if well done, it requires the reader to think about a **theme** in a way they have probably never done before.

Here is a sample answer exploring the **themes** of **music** and **friendship** from the 2019 exam paper using the example of a band playing on stage. Can you identify the **description** and **reveal** sections?

> The feel of the steel strings beneath my fingertips, vibrating as I strum my nails along them. The rhythm of the notes as I jump from chord to chord. This is what music really is, I would tell myself. I would look round at Al on bass, Ruth on drums, and Paul at the mic and think life couldn't get any better. But little did I know it would soon all come crashing down.
>
> (74 words)

Pick two examples of how the narrator describes playing guitar:

1. _____

2. _____

What part of the passage shows how the narrator feels they are at a high point emotionally?

1. _____

2. _____

The **key part** of this section now is to introduce some **tension** into the story. Look again at the last line of the example:

> But little did I know it would soon all come crashing down.

This line lets the reader know that this story will contain danger. They immediately wonder what will happen. **But do not give away the ending in the opening paragraph!** This should be revealed later in the story and only hinted at now. This technique is known as **foreshadowing**.

Let's work on an example on the **theme** of **fun** from the 2018 paper.

Think of something that you do for fun: _____

> Pick any activity that you do for fun, like running, dancing, sports, and so on.

Fun for me was always _____

_____

_____

> Describe two things you do when you are doing this activity. For running, you could say, 'The feel of my feet pounding the pavement mile after mile.'

But I never knew fear until _____

_____

_____

_____

> What could happen to take this activity away? What could stop the fun?

Time to Impress

For most … For me …

To learn another way to impress the reader and improve your **language** mark, look at this example from the **Everyone and then me** section earlier:

> For most, it is a time of joy and wonder, of magic and self-discovery. For me, it was a time of danger and difficulty, of self-doubt and recovery.

This is an interesting way to show contrast. Here's another one to practise with on the **theme** of **mystery**:

For most, their lives had mystery and _____, excitement and _____. For me, it was boredom and _____, dullness and _____.

Here's another on **success**:

For most, they experienced success and _____, glory and _____.
For me, it was failure and _____, defeat and _____.

Class/Homework exercise

- Here are some ideas for the **description and reveal** technique. Write down three things that someone does during an activity.

Example: Looking at my phone:

1. Scrolling through my friends' feeds.

2. Liking photos.

3. Posting pics.

1. Playing football	5. Chatting with friends in a café
2. Singing in the shower	6. Getting ready for a night out
3. Walking in the rain	7. Dancing with friends
4. Hiking in the mountains	8. Lying in bed, relaxing

Here are some **themes** that have come up in past exams.

- Firstly, **brainstorm** them.

- Then use the techniques you have learned in this lesson to write opening paragraphs about them.

1. Confusion (2019)	**6.** Kindness (2017)
2. Friends (2019)	**7.** Forgiveness (2017)
3. Health (2019)	**8.** Brothers/sisters (siblings) (2018)
4. Regret (2018)	**9.** Work (2018)
5. Pleasure (2017)	**10.** Tolerance (2016)

 Time to Reflect

1. How do you find the **theme** in a question?

2. Why is it important to know the **theme** before you plan and write an answer?

3. How does the **'everyone and then me'** way of beginning a story work? What is its aim?

4. What benefits do you think **description and reveal** brings to your writing?

5. Which of the two styles do you think works better?

6. Which of them would you use to write your story?

LESSON 23: SETTING

Learning Objectives – By the end of this lesson you should:

- Know why **setting** is vital in **creating a world** for the reader
- Know how to use your **senses** to create a **believable setting**
- Be able to write a **compelling setting paragraph** using **high-quality** language

 Time to Think

Ever wonder why some books and films feel more *real* than others? Sometimes it's because the setting is very similar to our own world, where we see people and places that we've seen our whole lives.

Can you think of a book you've read or a film you watched with a memorable setting? Was it realistic?

Let's take an example from a text that's regularly on the Leaving Certificate course:

> It was a bright cold day in April, and the clocks were striking thirteen. Winston Smith, his chin nuzzled into his breast in an effort to escape the vile wind, slipped quickly through the glass doors of Victory Mansions, though not quickly enough to prevent a swirl of gritty dust from entering along with him.

From *Nineteen Eighty-Four* by George Orwell

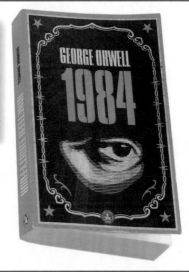

What do you think of the image of the eye on the cover? What kind of atmosphere does the idea that 'Big Brother is watching you' create for the book?

What kind of **setting** is created? Pick out words that describe the **mood**. Do you think this is an **engaging** and **descriptive** opening that grabs the reader's attention? Why?

It is so important to think about how you are going to **create the world** of your story if you want your reader, or the examiner, to feel they are a part of it.

PCLM

C – As a writer, you must show evidence of **planning** in your story. This includes creating a **setting** for your character to live in. This means that when something happens to them, the reader can picture it much better.

L – *How* you describe your **setting** is just as important as *what* you describe. The more detail you give of the world you are creating, the higher your mark will be. Using better vocabulary such as strong, interesting **verbs**, **adverbs**, and **adjectives** will help you do this.

Exploring setting

The easiest way to create a setting is with a **word bank**. This is done by simply writing down any word that comes to mind when you consider the location. This can be an object, an emotion, a description, or literally anything that comes into your head.

An easy way of thinking about it is to look at your physical senses:

- Sight
- Hearing
- Feeling (including touch and emotions)
- Smell
- Taste

In the 2019 paper, students were asked about a character whose determination to be the centre of attention has unexpected consequences. Here is a sample **setting** paragraph based around a school:

Feel

School was boring. From the (hard, plastic) seats that would murder your back to the teachers' droning voices, life could be hell there. And don't get me started about the smell. We were always beside the Science labs, and the chemicals would choke you. But there was Home Ec., I suppose. Miss would let us do up a gorgeous greasy fry every Friday – if we didn't annoy her (which wasn't often). Like I said, school was boring. Until the day Justin first showed up and made us all laugh.

(88 words)

Find an example of each of the **senses** and circle them in the paragraph. **Feeling/touch** is done already as an example.

Complete a sample **word bank** on the **gym** before writing your own paragraph. Fill in the extra spaces yourself:

1. Sight: Machines, muscles, people, shorts, and brightly coloured gym gear. Clear blue of a silent swimming pool. Runners, TV, spin bikes, sweat, red faces

   _____

2. Hearing: Heavy breathing. Feet on the treadmill. Splash of the water. Gasping for air. Bursting jet of water from a hydro pool

   _____

3. Feeling: Grip on the weights. Sweat on your forehead. Happy when the workout is done. Jealous of people fitter than you

   _____

4. Smell: Sweat, chlorine. Chalk from the grips on the weights. Scent of shower gel and wet hair

   _____

5. Taste: Energy drinks, protein shakes, bananas. Salty taste of sweat. Swallowing chlorinated water

   _____

Now let's pick another **setting** that everyone is familiar with: **a bakery**. Think of how your senses experience the setting and answer the questions below, in pairs or groups.

Make sure you use all of your senses when you are describing the bakery.

Sight: What would you see there? Don't just think of the obvious, like bread. Think of objects, people, clothes, stains, colours.

_____

_____

_____

Hearing: What noises would you hear? Would there be any constant noises, like a humming? What about bangs? What causes the noises? What speech would you hear?

_____

_____

Feeling: Think of the touch of the items in the bakery. What do they feel like? What about the temperature? Would it be cold? Warm? Both? Why? Also think of the texture of the food as you're eating it.

_____

_____

Smell: A bakery is a great source of smells. Again, don't focus on the easy ones, like baking bread. Think of the different ingredients. Or how would the bakery smell if something went wrong?

_____

_____

Taste: Now imagine eating the things in the bakery. What tastes good? Why? What tastes don't you like? Why?

_____

_____

Question analysis

Below are some of the same sample questions as the lesson on **theme**, but now we're going to look at them in a different way. Before, we were considering the **themes** only. But now we must think about where we could set our composition.

Tip For Success

Know your setting

In the pressure situation of an exam hall, it can be quite difficult to come up with brand-new ideas off of the top of your head. So, stick to what you know. When including a **setting** in your personal essay or short story, use a setting you already know and can describe in detail. Showing intimate knowledge – like what time of day the sun comes through the windows, or the sounds of the city or countryside you can hear from your bedroom – will make the **setting** far more realistic and will also improve your **language** mark.

You can have more than one setting, but don't go overboard. One or two well-described settings is more than enough.

Composing

In pairs or groups, look at the titles again and write down some places where you think you could set the story. You should also add in some story ideas. This can be hard to imagine the first few times you do it, so first try out some of your ideas with your classmates. Some examples have been done to show you.

> **1.** Write a short story where the main character undergoes a transformation. (Sample)

Gym (working hard to build up from being weak to strong).

School (going from a failing mark to getting the result you need for your course).

> **2.** Write a short story in which a group of childhood friends form what becomes a world-famous band but live to regret their success. (2019)

Local sports hall (meet up and practise until we get good).

> **3.** Write a personal essay in which you discuss what you have already achieved in life, and what you hope to achieve in the future. (2018)

Local area (coaching the local GAA team and want to win the championship).

> **4.** Write a short story which involves a race against time to prevent a disaster. (2018)

Nuclear power plant (meltdown is in progress, and I have to stop it).

> **5.** Write a personal essay giving your views on the importance of praise and encouragement as we go through life. (2017)

> **6.** Write a short story in which the main character goes on an exciting journey and learns some valuable lessons along the way. (2016)

 **Time to Write**

After we've explored the idea of **setting** and created a **word bank**, we must now look at the way we write about it. Look at this paragraph describing a gym:

There's more to the gym than just what you see. Make sure you use all of your senses to describe it.

I saw a man running on the treadmill. I saw people lifting weights. I heard music coming from the speakers. I felt my shirt stick to me. I smelled the sweat in the air. I tasted the water that I brought.

This paragraph contains a lot of description, but it is written badly. Describing a setting like this can turn it into a list and make it sound dull and uninteresting to the reader. Why is this, do you think?

- 'I' – Count how many times the word 'I' is used: _____ Do you need to write it so many times?

- **Repetitive sentence structure** – Look at the way the sentences are constructed: they are similar in length and each one tells us only one thing. How can you change the sentences so the story can flow from one sentence to the next?

- **Lack of adjectives** (words describing things) and **adverbs** (words describing actions) – What kind of a man is on the treadmill? Think of three descriptive words:

  _____

  How was he running? Think of another three:

  _____

  What will being creative with your language choice show the examiner?

- **Basic verb choice** – It says the music was 'coming' out of the speaker. This is a neutral verb like 'said' or 'went'. It just says what happens, but not how it happens. Choose three different verbs that could describe the music:

  _____

  What effect does choosing better verbs have on your writing?

So, let's have another look at the paragraph above. There are so many things that could have been described better. Some of them are circled. Write down as many words you can think of that describe these nouns:

I saw a man running on the treadmill. I saw people lifting (weights.) I heard (music) coming from the speakers. I felt my (shirt) stick to me. I smelled the sweat in the air. I tasted the (water) that I brought.

Weights: _____

_____

Music: _____

_____

Shirt: _____

_____

Composing

Water: _____

_____

Now use these descriptions to create a better **setting paragraph**. Here's the first part to get you started:

> Describe a person running on the treadmill. How big were they? What were they wearing?

As I entered the gym, the first thing that struck me was _____

_____

> Describe the way they ran. Was it loud? Were they sweaty? Did they grunt as they ran?

They were running so quickly that _____

_____

Time to Impress

Simile and comparison

You may decide to use a **simile** to bring further creativity to your writing. This is when you **compare** two different things using either 'like' – **He jumped out of the way of the car like a flash** – or 'as': **As quiet as a mouse, he crept into the room**. Showing how similar the two things are helps make your description far more vivid and clear for the reader.

Also, comparing things with 'more than' can help make your writing interesting: **Sasha wanted that designer dress more than she had every wanted anything in her life**.

The examples above are pretty common. You need to think of **similes** and **comparisons** that really make the reader think about what you want them to see and to look at things in a new and interesting way. Here are a few examples to get you started:

1. The lights on the tower shone like a million stars, each one twinkling like a diamond on a wedding ring.

2. The ball flew through the air as majestically as a golden eagle swooping through the sky.

3. More than all the money in the world, Mohammad wanted to play for Liverpool.

Now you can work on the rest:

4. The car sped around the corner like _____

_____

5. The boat sailed across the blue sea like _____

_____

6. The music droned on like _____

_____

Now we will change the order, putting the simile first:

1. As if he had just been launched out of a fighter-jet ejector seat, Seán _____

_____

2. As if she had just seen water for the first time in weeks after a trek across the desert, Jasmine _____

_____

3. As a lioness would stalk its prey before pouncing, the boxer _____

_____

4. More than _____, Cillian desired _____

_____

Class/Homework exercise

Now that you have the idea of how to create a **word bank** using your **senses**, try out some of these scenes to improve your vocabulary. You can work in groups or on your own.

- A park during a summer's day
- A police station holding cell
- A dungeon in a castle
- A bank during a robbery
- A beauty salon the day of the Debs
- A stadium on the day of the All-Ireland/World Cup Final

Now, take the following '**bad**' setting paragraphs:

- Circle **four** things in each that could be described better
- Write out **three better descriptions** for each thing
- Now, write a **better version** of the paragraph

1. **Famous landmark:** The Eiffel Tower shone at night time. I arrived when it got dark. I walked up to it. It was big. The lights were bright.
2. **Haunted house:** The room was cold. There was a window that was open. The bed was unmade. I went in. Then I saw it. I was afraid.
3. **Phoenix Park:** The sun was shining. I walked across the grass. The deer were grazing. I looked at their antlers. They were lovely.
4. **Concert:** The lights went down. The crowd cheered. I was excited. The band came on. The music began.

 Time to Reflect

1. Why is creating an interesting **setting** important in a story?
2. What **impact** does it have on the reader?
3. List the **five senses** that you could use to describe a place.
4. Think of two reasons why you should always **share ideas** with your partner, in a pair or as a group.
5. Why is it important **not to be repetitive** when using sentence structure?
6. Do you think using an **original simile** is effective? Would you use one in your own writing?

LESSON 24: CHARACTER CREATION

Learning Objectives – By the end of this lesson you should:

- Understand the importance of **character creation** in a piece of writing
- Be able to describe a **character's appearance** in a creative way
- Be able to describe a **character's personality** using **anecdotes**

 Time to Think

Often, when we watch a film or read a book, we are rooting for the hero. We want them to defeat the odds and to save the world. They go through all the difficulties the bad guys put in front of them, and we want them to succeed. But why is that? Why don't we care about the henchmen that are disposed of on the hero's journey to victory?

Think about the amount of time on screen or in a novel a hero character is given before something bad happens to them. We know who they are and have seen them grow as a person. Why does this make us more likely to care what happens?

Here's an example of **character creation** which shows how to create a striking first impression:

> Lord Asriel was a tall man with powerful shoulders, a fierce dark face, and eyes that seemed to flash and glitter with savage laughter. It was a face to be dominated by, or to fight: never a face to patronize or pity. All his movements were large and perfectly balanced, like those of a wild animal, and when he appeared in a room like this, he seemed a wild animal held in a cage too small for it.

From *Northern Lights* by Philip Pullman

James McAvoy as Lord Asriel in the BBC adaption of Northern Lights.

What words in the opening sentence show how commanding this character is? What does his face show about his personality? What **simile** is used in the last sentence? How effective is it at showing this person's character? These kinds of descriptions make the reader care about your character and whether they want them to win or to lose.

Tip For Success

Using adjectives

Using **adjectives** enhances your work and shows off your vocabulary, raising your **language** mark. However, we often only use the most basic adjectives as they are the first to pop into our heads. When we are describing someone, we might say 'a great guy' or 'a smart girl'. But you know way more adjectives than you think you do.

For 'great,' you could have said: wonderful, amazing, quality, super, fantastic, extraordinary.

For 'smart,' you could say: sharp, intelligent, bright, brainy, clued-in, savvy.

The first word that comes into your head is usually not the most descriptive or accurate one, so have a think to see if you can come up with a better one.

For example, if you were describing someone, can you think of more interesting adjectives you could use instead of 'funny'?

Exploring character creation

So, when you are describing a character for your personal essay or short story, there are two main ways to do so:

1. Appearance
2. Personality

Each aspect of **character creation** builds a picture of the person you are creating. It makes them more rounded and realistic. Remember, you will have already created a **setting** for them to live in, so now it is important to make the characters as lifelike as possible. Here's an example of a character's **appearance**:

His hair was the kind of black that you only saw in L'Oréal ads. It shone when the sunlight bounced off it during those warm summer days. Occasionally, he would smile. Not very often, but when he did, it lit up the room he was in. The intensity of his dark eyes would draw you in like a black hole. You couldn't escape from them.

(65 words)

1. Circle the three things about the boy that are described in the paragraph.

2. How is the character's hair described? _____
   _____

3. How is the contrast between light and dark shown in the paragraph?
   _____
   _____
   _____

   Definition
   Contrast: means how two things are different. Another word for it is '**juxtaposition**'.

4. What **simile** is used in the second last sentence? _____
   _____

Here's another example, but this time it is for **personality**. Make sure that whatever character trait you choose to describe is important to the narrative you are going to tell. Look for an **anecdote** which shows the character acting as they are described:

Remember: an anecdote is a little story that shows a moment when a character acts like the word you've used to describe them: **She was sporty and was on the Ireland hockey squad.**

Would you get angry if someone splashed you like this? What does it tell us about the character's personality that she gets so annoyed?

One thing you need to know about Aoibh was that her temper was legendary. To those who only met her, she looked, and acted, perfectly normal. That was until someone got in her way.

Last summer we all went swimming at the National Aquatic Centre. It was all going great until some girl splashed Aoibh when trying to get her mate. It looked like an accident, but not to Aoibh. It took three of us to drag her away, and, no, we haven't been back since.

(86 words)

1. What aspect of the **character's personality** is the paragraph describing? _____
   _____

2. Briefly explain what the **anecdote** was about. _____
   _____

3. What does this tell us about her as a person? _____
   _____

Let's have another look at some past exam questions and begin to create some characters that you could use in these stories. One is a **short story** and the other is a **personal essay**.

Write a **short story** which involves a race against time to prevent a disaster. (2018)

For a **short story**, you can write in the **first person** (I) or in the **third person** (she/he/it); so you can either invent a character or use yourself as a starting point. It doesn't have to be the *real* you. You are allowed to change and add things to make the description suit the question. For this dramatic story, you will need to decide: are they a regular person who must leave their comfort zone to save the day? Or are they a true action hero like The Rock or Jason Statham?

Write a **personal essay** in which you discuss what you have already achieved in life and what you hope to achieve in the future. (2018)

The **personal essay** is much more reflective. You will need to think about the things you have achieved so far in your life. What parts of your character have driven you to achieve them? What do you want to do in the future?

Firstly, we'll focus on **appearance**. Think of aspects of a character's **body** that you could describe:

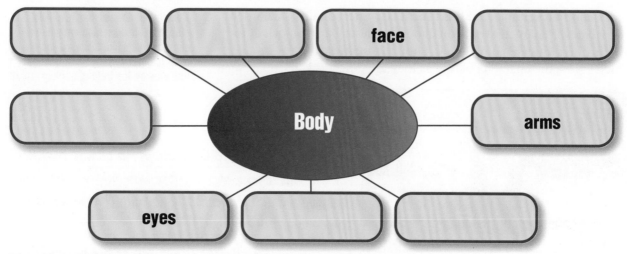

The other part of **appearance** is much more personal. Think about the **fashion choices** or **accessories** a person could have – or physical things, like scars.

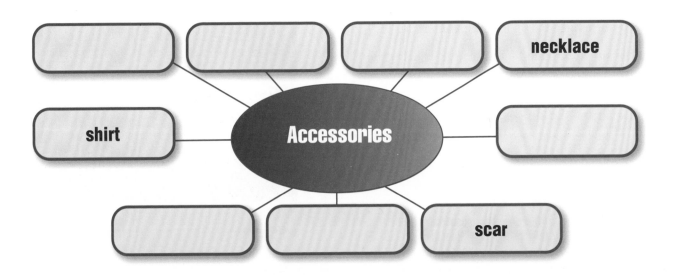

Accessories

- shirt
- necklace
- scar

Now you need to create a **word bank**. Choose **two** of your words from **body** and **accessories** and think of as many words as you can to describe them:

Body: Face –
1. Beautiful, with nice skin
2. Ugly
3. Big and round
4. Long and sad

Body: _____ –
1. _____
2. _____
3. _____
4. _____

Body: _____ –
1. _____
2. _____
3. _____
4. _____

Accessories: Shirt –
1. Newest fashion
2. Old and torn
3. Football jersey
4. Tight and muscular

Accessories: _____ –
1. _____
2. _____
3. _____
4. _____

Accessories: _____ –
1. _____
2. _____
3. _____
4. _____

Time to Write

Once you've decided on the kind of character you are going to create, it's time to start bringing them to life. The key part is making sure they are realistic, and that they suit the story you are trying to tell.

In a short story and a personal essay, you will need **two** main characters:

- The **protagonist** – the main character in the story who has to overcome an obstacle to succeed.

- The **antagonist** – someone (or something) that gets in the **protagonist's** way and tries to stop them succeeding. The **antagonist** is usually a person, but sometimes can be represented by a thing: an injury, an animal, or an event such as a natural disaster. It can even be **inside the protagonist** themselves – a fear or anxiety that is stopping them achieving their goal. Whatever suits the story.

Hugh Jackman as Jean Valjean and Russell Crowe as Javert in Les Misérables. *Who is the protagonist and who is the antagonist in the story?*

Many stories also have a third character:

- The **sidekick/friend** – this character helps the **protagonist** succeed through advice or encouragement.

So let's create a sample **protagonist** for the disaster story question from the 2018 exam paper. He is a regular guy, who will have to do something extraordinary to save the day.

Ron Weasley and Hermione Grainger: Harry Potter's friends and sidekicks.

Appearance – Body

> What does short, neat hair tell us about Will? How does it show he is 'a regular guy'?

Will was just a regular guy. His hair was short and neat. This always told me that _____
_____
_____

> Describe how his face was regular. How could he just blend in?

His face was _____
_____
_____

But what stood out were his arms. They were _____
_____

> How did his arms stand out? Were they skinny? Powerful?

In pairs, write **two reasons** why is it important to the story that the character seems normal.

1. _____
_____

2. _____
_____

Appearance – Accessories

You would never see him without his hoodie. It was _____
_____
_____

> Describe the hoodie. Was it new or old? Ripped? What design was on it? Be as descriptive as possible. Why would wearing it show how regular he was?

This always told us that _____
_____
_____

> What does this item of clothing tell us about the character? Link it to the paragraph you just wrote on Appearance – Body.

Personality – Anecdote

To be honest, Will was the most regular, ordinary person I think ever
existed. In school, all of his test results were _____

_____

_____

I remember last year, during the heatwave, he still went around in _____

_____

_____

Once, Mr O'Leary let us go home an hour early. All of us screamed with
joy as we ran out the gates. Well, all of us bar Will. He _____

_____

_____

_____

> What results are the most 'regular' you can think of?

> How do you think Will dressed in the heat? Was it any different to his usual clothes?

> How was the way Will left school early different to the rest of his classmates? Was it any different to how he usually left school?

With your **protagonist** created, you then have to think about your **antagonist** and how to bring **conflict** into the story. What is **challenging** the protagonist? What is **getting in their way**? As described earlier, the **antagonist** in your story can be a person, an event, or a thing. Remember Alice Stone, the comedian in the comedy club in **Lesson 21** (page 111)? Who was her antagonist? How did her antagonist create conflict for Alice? What choice did Alice have to make?

In this sample answer, instead of having an antagonist who is a person, our antagonist is a thing. The personal essay question mentioned earlier from the 2018 paper asks you to describe things you want to achieve in the future. Let's look at what can get in your way.

Imagine that what you want to achieve is to **travel the world**. List **five** things that could stop you from doing this:

1. Afraid I will be homesick.

2. Worried I might not fit in in the places I visit.

3. _____

4. _____

5. _____

Now create a paragraph describing this **antagonist** and the **conflict or challenge** they create for you:

I've always wanted to travel the world. This is a huge goal of mine, but one I feel is out of
reach. The main reason is _____

> Choose a reason from your list.

> **Explain in detail using an example how this has always held you back.**

It has always held me back because _____

_____

_____

But I'm not going to let this stop me forever. What I really need to do to overcome this is

_____

_____

_____

> **Describe what you need to do to overcome this antagonist/challenge.**

 ## Time to Impress

No one loved _____ as much as …

A useful way to show how a character is unique is to pick a particular part of their personality that only they show. Just make sure the characteristic links in with the story.

No one loved summer as much as Paddy. Every year, from the day we came back to school after the Christmas holidays, he would count down the days in his journal to the day school finished for the summer holidays. It was tradition at this point for him to ring at 7 a.m. on the last day to scream, 'Happy summer!' down the phone at me.

(66 words)

Now you can try some. Finish the following examples:

> **How often would she sing? Would she film herself? How many likes would she get? What did the audience think?**

We all knew no one loved singing as much as Sophie. From the age of three, she would _____

_____

_____

> **How often would Dylan talk about films? How many times a week did he go to the cinema? What did other people think about his obsession with film?**

It was clear that no one loved films as much as Dylan. Every day he _____

_____

_____

- Look at the following list of character traits. Choose **five** and write an **anecdote** about each description:

1. Lonely	8. Intelligent	15. Artistic
2. Stubborn	9. Wise	16. Powerful
3. Angry	10. Ignorant	17. A leader
4. Fiery	11. Helpful	18. A follower
5. Odd	12. Destructive	19. Delightful
6. Athletic	13. Well-dressed	20. Bored
7. Sly	14. Confident	21. Timid

- Take these two past exam questions and come up with a **protagonist** and an **antagonist**.

> You can use the protagonist, Will, created earlier as a starting point, or create an entirely new protagonist. What or who will your antagonist be?

1. Write a short story which involves a race against time to prevent a disaster. (2018)

2. Write a personal essay giving your views on the importance of praise and encouragement as we go through life. (2017)

- Describe both your **protagonist** and your **antagonist** fully by describing their:

- Appearance – Body

- Appearance – Accessories

- Personality – Anecdote

▷◁ Time to Reflect

1. Why is it important to develop a **character** early in your story?

2. List **five** ways you can describe a character's body.

3. What is a **protagonist**?

4. What is an **antagonist**?

5. What is the point of using an **anecdote** to show a person's personality?

Learning Objectives – By the end of this lesson you should:

- Understand the importance of **word choice**
- Know why it's important for a character to have a **high point**
- Be able to write an **action** scene

 Time to Think

About thirty minutes into most films, it usually looks like everything is going great for the main character. Life seems good. Then, it happens: their world begins to fall apart around them. Why do you think the writer or director shows you the character at their **high point** before bringing them down?

Often this turning point happens in a very dramatic scene. In the film *Taken*, it's the scene in which the main character's daughter is kidnapped. In *Frozen*, it's when Elsa runs away because she can't control her powers. In *Of Mice and Men*, it's Lennie killing Curley's wife. In pairs, think of a few more examples from films you've seen and novels you've read.

So how do you write this dramatic **action** scene? Here's an example from an author based in Ireland who writes in the sci-fi/fantasy genre.

> With a loud shriek, an arrow flew through the air and struck the [other] warrior. Ragnok Strongarm was making no effort to cross to his opponent, but had calmly strung his bow and was watchfully preparing his next shot … Another shrieking missile. The warrior was struck mid-leap and spun into the water. He disappeared and did not come up.

From *Epic* by Conor Kostick

The cover of Epic *by Conor Kostick. Is there anything in the image that may hint at what the plot will be?*

How did the author show that the **action** had begun? How was **tension** created? Look again at the description of the final shot. Why does it work so well?

PCLM

C – It is important for your **plot** and **character development** that you show how things are **going well** before **disaster** strikes. It means the reader will care more.

L – You need to show the examiner your ability to **describe action events**, so make them as detailed as possible.

Exploring action

High point

So, what should a **high point** contain and how do you write one? The key element is **optimism**. The reader should feel that everything is going well for the character. This makes us feel sorry for them when it all goes badly in the **action scene**. Here is an example for the race against time to prevent a disaster question from the 2018 paper:

It all seemed like a (dream come true) for Emily: the golden sands between her toes as she walked; the lapping sound of the waves against the shore; the feel of the warm breeze on her skin. The world could not get any sweeter than this. A smile spread across her face as she closed her eyes and took a deep, soothing breath. 'Bliss,' she murmured to herself.

(68 words)

1. Where does the scene take place? _____

2. How does the writer show that the character realises they are happy and lost in the moment?

   _____

3. Circle **four** words or phrases in the paragraph that show the character is enjoying herself. One is done for you.

4. Why is it important that the author shows how happy the character is? _____

   _____

5. What mood is created in the paragraph? _____

   _____

Action

Once the **high point** is created, the plot moves on to the **action scene** where you should show how good turns to bad. It needs to be very descriptive and capture the reader's attention.

Then it hit her. Before Emily could even process what had happened, she was in the air, her eyes no longer looking at the shimmering sea, but at the beautiful blue sky. A moment later, she hit the sand and heard a sickening crack. An explosion of pain shot up through her left arm straight up into her shoulder. But before she even had a chance to scream, a growl and snarl caught her attention. Vicious (fangs) were inches from her face. The danger was not over.

(87 words)

How would you feel if you saw this bearing down on you?

1. What has happened to the woman? _____

   _____

2. It never says the word, 'dog' in the paragraph. Circle **three** words from the example that show it was a dog who ran into her. One is done for you.

3. How has the mood changed from the **high point**? Explain. _____

   _____

4. How do we know the character was shocked by what happened? _____

   _____

The **action** scene doesn't have to be one where there's a fight or a disaster. It could also be a conversation where someone says something they shouldn't or delivers news that turns the character's world upside down. Below is a sample paragraph from the 'praise and encouragement' personal essay asked for in the 2017 exam paper, in which the character's parents always push them to be the best they could be.

Everything seemed perfect, but the next morning, my whole world was rocked. I came down for my breakfast, and my parents were sitting at the table holding hands. This in itself set alarm bells off in my mind. They were always at work by the time I rolled out of bed and descended zombie-like down the stairs. But here they were, and you only had to look at their faces to know that the news wasn't going to be good. The envelope with the hospital logo on the front of it said it all.

(94 words)

1. How does the author shift the mood in this scene? Focus on the opening line.

   _____

2. Before we know what's wrong, how does the author hint that something bad has happened?

   _____

3. How does the author use **foreshadowing** in the last sentence?

   _____

   _____

Question analysis

As part of your planning for writing a short story or a personal essay, you need to think about **plot development**. How does the story show what was once good has now turned bad?

Look at these past exam questions. Think of a **high point** and then an **action scene** that moves the **plot** on.

Tip For Success

Is it important to the question?

When you are writing your **action scene**, you must make sure that what you include **relates to the question**. Just because you want to write in a car chase or a huge row between two characters caught in a love triangle, it doesn't mean that it fits in with what the question asks you.

In 2019, there was a **short story question** about a character who wants to be the centre of attention – so the action should take place in front of a group. A personal essay question in the 2018 paper was about having siblings – so include a fight between you and your brother or sister. Make sure that the **dramatic point** in your composition is **important to the question**.

1. Write a short story in which a group of childhood friends form what becomes a world-famous band but live to regret their success. (2019)

High point – We've just had a number one song and a sold-out tour.

Action – An argument with my bandmates because I want to go solo and fame has gone to my head.

2. Write a personal essay in which you discuss what you think your life would be like if you were unable to use any form of social media for a whole year. (2019)

High point – I just got a new phone for Christmas, and I'm loving spending my life on social media.

Action – A conversation with my dad where he says he'll give me €1,000 if I go without my phone for a year. Only reason I'd do it!

---

3. Write a short story which involves a race against time to prevent a disaster. (2018)

High point – I'm delighted to be on my way to see my aunt who I haven't seen in years.

Action – A car crash happens in front of us and _____

_____

> What must you do to save the day? What is the race against time?

High point – _____

_____

Action – _____

_____

> Work out the **high point** and **action scene** for the **protagonist** and **antagonist** you created for this question in Lesson 24 (page 135).

---

4. Write a personal essay in which you discuss what you have already achieved in life and what you hope to achieve in the future. (2018)

High point – I've worked so hard to achieve _____

_____

_____

> What did you achieve? How do you feel about it?

Action – Fighting with my local TD on RTÉ radio _____

_____

> What did the TD do or say? Why are you challenging him?

---

5. Write a personal essay giving your views on the importance of praise and encouragement as we go through life. (2017)

High point – _____

_____

Action – _____

_____

> Use the protagonist and antagonist you created in **Lesson 24** (page 135) for this exercise. How does creating **a high point** and **action scene** for these characters move the story along?

6. Write a short story in which the main character goes on an exciting journey and learns some valuable lessons along the way. (2016)

High point – _____

_____

_____

Action – _____

_____

_____

 Time to Write

Now that you have some ideas for plotting out your story or essay, it's time to start writing. First of all, you must set up your **high point**. Let's take the giving up social media personal essay question from 2019 that you worked on in the section above (question 2 on page 138).

High point

I just got a new phone for Christmas, and I'm loving spending my life on social media.

> Name some social media apps that you might use.

My phone is the access point to my life. With one tap, I can open _____

_____

> What would you see on these apps? Why does it make you happy to see these things?

The joy it gives me to see _____

_____

_____

It might mean that I don't _____

_____

These things don't really matter to me, but they do to my dad.

> What kinds of things would you miss out on if you only looked at social media? Think about times you were looking at your phone when around other people.

With the **high point** completed, you can now create the **action**. For this we will look at the 'prevent a disaster' question from the 2018 paper which you worked on earlier. Here your **high point** describes a car crash:

How is a sense of speed created in the image?

High point

I'm delighted to be on my way to see my aunt who I haven't seen in years.

What kinds of things could you hear? The engine? The wheels? Describe the sounds.

I could hear it before I saw it. _____
_____

The Porsche couldn't avoid the kerb. Its back wheel clipped it, and _____
_____
_____

Describe the explosion of the wheel. Where did the rubber go? The smell of it?

Finally, the vehicle sped into the wall with a sickening smash. The sight was awful; the bonnet _____, the windscreen _____, the driver _____
_____

Describe in only a few words how the bonnet, the windscreen, and the driver looked after the crash.

The last sample we will work on is where the **action scene** takes place during a **conversation**. For this one, we'll use the personal essay question from 2018 where you talk about what you've achieved in life (4. on page 139). The **action scene** will be your **conversation on live radio** with the TD.

High point

I've worked so hard to achieve

_____
_____

What was the TD saying about your area? The people? The schools?

But the great day I was having was ruined when my mam turned on the car radio on the way home. Here was John Reilly, our local TD, saying our area was
_____
_____
_____

I could feel my anger rising. My face _____, my heart rate _____, my fists _____.

I grabbed my phone out of my pocket, rang the station's number, and told him _____
_____

Describe how this anger showed. What happened the colour of your face? What happened to the speed and thump of your heart rate? What did you do with your fists?

What did you tell the TD? Refer to the things he said earlier.

Composing

 **Time to Impress**

Slow motion

Think of any American high school drama you've ever seen. The basketball team is two points down, and the star player has the ball in his hands. There is less than a second to go. He lines up the three-pointer and, all of a sudden, the whole world slows down. You see the ball rotate in the air. You see the crowd's reactions. You see the coach's face. You hear the gasp as it hits the rim.

But once it drops in, we are back to real time for the celebrations. Something that takes less than a second in real life, can take about a minute on film. Writers do that as well. It creates **tension** and **suspense**, and showcases your writing ability. Here is an example:

Real time

Pascal picked up a bottle and threw it across the classroom. The teacher opened the door at the wrong moment, and it hit him in the face.

(27 words)

Slow motion

Pascal arched backwards, gripping the full bottle firmly. The potential energy was massive, like a bowstring pulled so far back it marked the archer's fingers. He released the bottle so that it rotated sweetly in the air. The massive riot around him stopped as everyone watched the (heavy) bottle journey majestically across the room. We could see the final destination, but none of us could stop it. Mr Hayes was talking to the Maths teacher and not paying attention. He turned just as the bottle loudly smacked into his face. The awful sound. We had gone too far.

(98 words)

It is important to be as detailed as possible and use adjectives (which describe things) and adverbs (which describe actions). Reread the above passage and:

1. Circle the **adjectives**

2. Highlight or underline the **adverbs**

One of each has already been marked to start you off.

Now look at the following example:

Real time

I heard my name and (walked up) onto the stage. I looked at all the faces as I collected my graduation cert. Then I sat back down, smiling.

(28 words)

1. Circle the actions in the example that could be described better. One is done for you already.

2. Take the example of 'walked up.' How did the narrator feel as they walked? _____

    _____

3. Think of one of the faces they saw on the way. What did it look like? Happy? Disappointed? Give a reason why it could look this way. _____

    _____

Now write the **slow motion** version.

Think about what would go through the head of the person receiving their graduation certificate after finally finishing their years in school.

> Describe the walk. How did the narrator feel making it? What could they see?

Slow motion

The whole world seemed to slow down as I heard my name. The walk up to the stage took forever as

_____

_____

I saw my mam in the crowd. She looked _____

_____

_____

> Describe their mam's face. Pick out the little details. Why would she have this expression?

The cheer of the crowd was like _____

_____

_____

> What feeling would the cheer give the narrator? How did their body react to it? Goosebumps? Chills? Tears of joy welling?

As I sat down, the world sped up again. But it was a moment I'd never forget.

Class/Homework exercise

Take the following examples and write **action scenes** for them using the skills you developed in this lesson. Don't forget to use **slow motion**:

1. Someone stealing your phone
2. Getting called to the principal's office
3. Your coach dropping you from the team
4. Getting grounded for something you didn't do
5. Forgetting your lines in the school play
6. Getting an injury in a big game
7. Receiving bad news about a loved one
8. Telling a friend you are moving away
9. Losing your notes the moment before the big debate
10. Waking up late for your flight and rushing to the airport

 ## Time to Reflect

1. Why is important to use interesting words and descriptions?

2. Why should your story have a **high point**? Why does it need an **action scene**?

3. What two kinds of **action scene** have you practised in this lesson?

4. How can you write an **action scene** that only has talking?

5. Why can writing a **real time** paragraph leave out description?

6. What benefits does a **slow motion** paragraph give to your work?

LESSON 26: TURNING POINT

Learning Objectives – By the end of this lesson you should:

- Know how to use **emotion** in a story or essay
- Understand how the **low point** works
- Know how to write a **turning point** and describe its **impact**

 Time to Think

Can you remember any examples of a film you've watched or a book you've read where the world seems to be weighing down the **protagonist** or where they feel it is impossible for them to succeed?

But then there is always a point where they turn it around. Something will happen that inspires them to move forward, get out of that dark emotional place, and finally be victorious. There are lots of examples in film and literature of this happening. Can you think of any? Why does the writer want to show us the character we have followed throughout the story being beaten down, emotionally or physically or both, before turning it around?

Here is an example of a **low point** from a text that is regularly on the Leaving Certificate. In it, Macbeth has just been told that his wife is dead:

> All our yesterdays have lighted fools
>
> The way to dusty death. Out, out, brief candle!

Macbeth, Act 5, Scene 5

Michael Fassbender in a film version of Macbeth.

Why do you think Macbeth calls his enemies 'fools'? The candle is a metaphor for life. What does the final line tell us about what's going on in Macbeth's head?

Macbeth's **turning point** is shown in this line:

> I am in blood
>
> Stepp'd in so far that, should I wade no more,
>
> Returning were as tedious as go o'er.

Macbeth, Act 3, Scene 4

The river of blood is a metaphor for all the murders Macbeth has committed. What does this line tell us about Macbeth? Having your character go through pain and turmoil is important as it lets the reader know a lot more about them as a person than if things were always perfect.

Patrick Stewart playing Macbeth in a modern interpretation of the play.

PCLM

C – It's important for the **structure** of your story that the narrator or character faces difficulty before finally overcoming it. This **turning point** leads into the **climax** where the difficulty is resolved.

L – This is a chance to show your writing ability by using **emotion** in your story or essay.

Exploring the turning point

There are many key **emotional** points in a composition. We have already looked at the **high point** where it looks like everything is going really well for your character. Then the **action scene** happens, and your character suffers. Now we have to show them at their **low point**.

Here is a sample paragraph answering the question in the 2019 paper about a character who likes to be the centre of attention.

Justin has reached the first round of *Britain's Got Talent*, but at the all-crucial moment, he's forgotten part of the routine he's performing.

It was at this point that Justin stopped smiling. He used to do his best to make us happy, to keep a bit of fun going. But no more. The failure under the glare of a spotlight had ruined him. The once bright light that shone in his eyes had gone out. His shoulders slumped as he dragged himself off the stage that night. There wasn't even a sympathy clap. Maybe he wasn't able to handle being the centre of attention after all.

(83 words)

1. What was the character like before the low point? _____

   _____

2. What happened that changed this? _____

   _____

3. How are his eyes described? _____

   _____

4. What does that tell you about what happened to him? _____

   _____

5. Look at how short the sentences are. How do short sentences reflect how sad a character is? _____

   _____

So, after we show the character suffering, we then have to show them getting their confidence back. There has to be a shift in **emotion** as it goes from **sad to optimistic**. You have to make it look like things can only get better from here.

That was when Simon Cowell shocked everyone and left his seat. He walked up right up to Justin. I don't think anyone had ever seen him do this before. 'Look, Justin, you passed the auditions; you made us all smile with your talent, and this was just one mistake. Go up and try again. You can do it.'

(58 words)

Imagine you were on stage and nothing was going right for you. How would you feel? How would you react?

1. In your own words, what did Simon say to Justin? _____

   _____

   _____

2. Why was it so surprising that he would say this? _____

   _____

   _____

Composing

Once you've created the character's **turning point**, you need to tell the reader what **impact** it had on the character.

Standing at the side of stage, I could see Justin's whole face lift. The spark was back! I could have talked all day, and it would have meant little, but all it took was a few encouraging words from Simon Cowell and Justin was back to his brilliant best. He stormed back onto the stage and wowed the audience. There were tears by the end of his performance. The good kind.

(71 words)

1. What impact did Simon Cowell's words have on the character? _____

    _____

    _____

2. Why do you think that only Simon's words could have had the impact they did? Why not the narrator's? _____

    _____

3. Look at the verb in 'He **stormed** back onto the stage.' What does this verb tell you about how Justin went back on stage? What does it tell us about the impact of Simon's words? _____

    _____

    _____

Question analysis

Here are some past exam **Composition** questions. What you need to do is figure out what the **low point** could be and give an example of how the character can turn it around.

> 1. Write a short story about a character whose determination to be the centre of attention has unexpected consequences. (2019)

Start with Justin's story from the section above:

Low point – Fails on stage and feels terrible.

Turning point – Gets encouragement from a famous judge to give it another go.

Impact – Wows the audience and gets through to the next round.

> 2. Write a short story in which a group of childhood friends form what becomes a world-famous band but live to regret their success. (2019)

Low point – Leaves the band to go solo but fails to get a hit song.

Turning point – Gets a call to go back to the band.

Little Mix are one of the most popular girl groups in the world today. Do you think it would be difficult to cope with that level of fame?

Impact – _____

_____

_____

> **3.** Write a personal essay in which you discuss what you have already achieved in life and what you hope to achieve in the future. (2018)

Low point – At first the pressure of the Junior Cycle exams was getting to me.

Turning point – _____

_____

Impact – _____

_____

_____

> **4.** Write a short story which involves a race against time to prevent a disaster. (2018)

Low point – The timer had nearly run out, and I was still trapped in the building.

Turning point – _____

_____

Impact – _____

_____

_____

> **5.** Write a personal essay giving your views on the importance of praise and encouragement as we go through life. (2017)

Low point – _____

_____

Turning point – _____

_____

_____

Impact – _____

_____

_____

6. Write a short story in which the main character goes on an exciting journey and learns some valuable lessons along the way. (2016)

Low point – _____

_____

Turning point – _____

_____

_____

Impact – _____

_____

_____

Time to Write

Once you've decided what your **low point**, **turning point**, and **impact** is going to be, you can then start to write your paragraphs. Why do you think using **emotive** language is so important here?

Let's take the 'already achieved in life' personal essay question from the 2018 paper. The **low point** suggested was the pressure of the Junior Cycle exams.

Tip For Success

Length of sentences

We looked at the use of full stops back in **Lesson 1**, but they are very important when you are speaking emotionally. For example, if a character is sad, or if a narrator is speaking about something painful, then make your sentences short and make sure you use full stops often.

On the other hand, if you are trying to show excitement or panic, having your sentences run a little longer than usual is a good way of reflecting this. But don't go overboard. Paragraphs that have sentences without full stops are a nightmare for examiners.

> List off some of the daily pressures of the Junior Cycle exams.

I'm going to be honest; the pressure of the Junior Cycle exams was getting to me. Every day it was _____

_____

Then when I got home, my dad would say _____

> What could the narrator's dad say that would heap extra pressure on?

_____

The daily grind was wearing me down and making me feel _____

_____

> Sum up how the narrator feels at their lowest point.

Then you can move onto the **turning point**. What happens to the character to make them turn it all around?

> How can seeing someone at their best while you feel overwhelmed make you feel?

But one Monday night, my phone rang. It was Nadia. We hadn't spoken in months. I thought she had it all under control, so I couldn't stand _____

_____

What she said shocked me. She spoke softly and said, ` _____

_____

_____

> Was Nadia also facing the same struggles? What encouraging words could she give?

Now all there is to be done is to describe the **impact** Nadia's words had on your character.

> How does what Nadia revealed make the narrator feel better?

My world changed immediately. If she _____

_____

_____

I replied to Nadia, ` _____

_____

_____

> What might the narrator say back? Might they also offer words of encouragement?

Life was a whole lot better that it was five minutes before, and I had a new perspective and motivation to kick ass in the Junior Cert.

 Time to Impress

There are many ways to show how a character can be inspired to turn it all around and here are some to practise:

Positive words

If the character is down, then sometimes all it takes is a positive speech from someone to help inspire them.

That was when she spoke those words I would never forget: `Liam, I believe in you.' From that moment on I knew I could do just about anything.

I stepped up to take the penalty. My face said I couldn't do it. Everyone could see. That's when Isabelle said, ` _____

_____

_____

Negative words

Sometimes it's someone telling them that they *can't* do something, that they're not able for it, that inspires a character to succeed.

The boos echoed around the arena. They all wanted me to fail. Thousands of voices chanting, `You suck, you suck.' But I would show them. Their hate was my fuel.

'Look, Richie, I just don't think you're good enough to join the band,' Mr O'Keeffe said, a slight sneer on his face. I'd show him. Next year I would _____

_____

See something inspirational

Perhaps the character might see something that changes their views and inspires them?

Then I saw her push down all those nerves and sing. It was the sweetest sound. The whole room was silent as they listened. The applause at the end was deafening. Well, if she can overcome her shyness, so can I.

I didn't think I could get to the top of the hill. We had been hiking for hours and my feet were sore and swollen. That's when I saw _____

_____

Decide that you've had enough

Sometimes a character can inspire themselves when they've simply had enough.

Garreth had had enough. No more would he let people speak to him like that. All the names, the comments, the texts. It was time to change it all. Revenge would be sweet.

This really was the last straw. Never again would Samira let them make her feel _____

_____

Class/Homework exercise

- Look at the following **low points** and **brainstorm** how the character might feel.
- Write **turning points** for each of the **low points**. Try to use different **Time to Impress** techniques for each one.
- Finally, write a paragraph describing the **impact** the **turning point** had on the character.
1. Diane has just been sacked from her part-time job for something she didn't do.
2. Seamus has been grounded for coming home at 3 a.m. Now he will miss his girlfriend's 18th birthday party.
3. Karla tried to get funding from the council to build a new school hall but was refused.
4. Yvonne likes to wear clothes that other people might find odd and gets comments whenever she goes into town.
5. Stephen wants to hold his boyfriend's hand as he walks down the street but feels afraid of what might people might say.
6. Ryan is in a building he knows he shouldn't be in. He can hear guards down the hall. He is trapped.

 ## Time to Reflect

1. What is the reason a story has a **low point**?
2. Why is it important to write using **emotion** for this section?
3. Why should the sentences be short in a **low point**?
4. What is a **turning point**?
5. List the kinds of **turning point** you can have in a story.
6. Why is it important to explain the **impact** of the **turning point**?

LESSON 27: CLIMAX AND RESOLUTION

Learning Objectives – By the end of this lesson you should:

- Understand how the **climax** completes your **composition** and ties up your **plot**
- Know how **tension** creates **suspense** and how relief brings **resolution**
- Be able to write a **climax** scene

 Time to Think

Imagine going to the cinema, paying your money at the box office, sitting down for two hours, and then have the screen go blank with ten minutes to go.

How would you feel?

Now imagine the examiner when they correct a story that just stops. They watch as you create a setting, then create a character to live in it. They then see this character go through a range of emotions from highs to lows. They cheer as the character comes through all their difficulties. And just as it seems the plot will be **resolved**, out of nowhere, the story just ends. How would the examiner – or any reader – feel after all of this?

Whatever the plan was for your personal essay or the plot was for your story, here is where it is resolved. If it is a short story about preventing a disaster, here is where you or your character save the day. If it is a personal essay about the pleasure of life's lazy days, then here is where you tell the reader the lasting impact these days have in a busy world. Why is it so important to have **resolution** in your writing?

Here is a famous **climax** scene from a novel you may have studied during Junior Cycle. Lennie, a slow-witted man, is on the run after accidentally killing a woman. The **climax** of the story occurs when George performs the only humane resolution he can think of:

> And George raised the gun and steadied it, and he brought the muzzle of it close to the back of Lennie's head. The hand shook violently, but his face set and his hand steadied. He pulled the trigger. The crash of the shot rolled up the hills and rolled down again. Lennie jarred, and then settled slowly forward to the sand, and he lay without quivering.

From *Of Mice and Men* by John Steinbeck

Chris O'Dowd as Lennie and James Franco as George in the recent Broadway adaptation of Of Mice and Men.

Definition

Suspense: means bringing danger or mystery into your story. Make sure you **resolve** it (fix the danger or reveal the mystery) later in the story.

The **plot** was about how George helped Lennie throughout his life. How did the **climax** show this? How do we know George found it hard to do what was he believed was necessary? How does the writer build **suspense**? How is the **tension relieved**?

Composing

P – You must be able to show that you have fully answered the question. The **climax** of the story or essay is where you show you have done this.

C – Structure is vital in story and essay writing. This is the final section. By having all sections of a **short story** or **personal essay**, it shows that your piece of writing is well planned.

Exploring the climax and resolution

When writing the **climax scene**, you need to go back and have another look at your plan. For the world-famous band question from the 2019 paper, the **climax** could be how the band gets back together after realising that success isn't all it's made out to be.

We had lived through the highs and lows. I regretted how the success had made me a monster. It turned me against the people I loved the most: the rest of the guys in the band. They were there for me when I needed them and, now, I wanted to repay that. When we stepped out on to the stage that night, the crowd screamed. I looked at Nadia, and she stared back at me. Then she hit the C chord on the guitar and smiled. The arena went wild. We were back.

(93 words)

1. Reread the first two sentences. How do they **link** back to what has happened already in the story?

    _____

2. The words 'regret their success' is in the question. Circle the words 'regretted' and 'success' in the paragraph.

3. The **climax** relieves the **tension** built up during the story. There was tension between the narrator and Nadia in the story. How do we know that it is relieved? _____

    _____

4. The **climax** usually finishes on a happy or positive note. Does this example? _____

    Explain why you think this. _____

    _____

    _____

Once the **climax** and **resolution** is written, all your story or essay needs is an **ending**. This is usually short and hints at what will happen next to the narrator or character. It also shows how they have developed as a person through overcoming the challenges and obstacles they have faced.

Night after night, the audiences went wild for us. It was like we had never been away. I learned a lot about myself from that year going solo. Although I might have regretted our success at the start, and the horrible person I became because of it, I know now that it turned me into the better person I am today.

(61 words)

How would you feel if you walked out to this kind of reaction, especially after going through so much in your story? Relieved? Vindicated?

1. Reread the first sentence. How does it show time has passed since the **climax**? _____

   _____

2. From what they say in this paragraph, how has the narrator grown as a person? _____

   _____

Tip For Success

Linking it all back to the question

By the end of a composition question, chances are that you have been writing for over an hour. You will be tired, both mentally and physically, at this point. But, unfortunately, the examiner doesn't care about this. All they care about is whether you answered the question or not.

This means that in the **climax** and **resolution** section of the composition, you must refer back to the question. This lets the examiner know that you were answering the question, even if you might have wandered off-topic at times.

Question analysis

It is really important to plan out your **climax** scene before you start writing. This means that your composition will always be heading towards an end point. All you need to do as a writer is to think of that final scene in your story where it all comes together. As you are writing, new ideas might come into your head and you can change parts of the plan. Why do you think it's helpful to have an end point in mind at the start?

Once you have your **climax scene** planned, you just need to think about what happens after the story is over. Will the protagonist live happily ever after? Will they change their ways? Has preventing the disaster changed who they are as a person? Readers love to know what happens after they finish the story, so let them know in the **ending**.

Here are some past exam questions to work on:

1. Write a short story in which a group of childhood friends form what becomes a world-famous band but live to regret their success. (2019)

Climax/resolution & ending – The band gets back together, and we go on stage one more time. The crowd goes wild for us.

2. Write a personal essay in which you discuss what you think your life would be like if you were unable to use any form of social media for a whole year. (2019)

Climax/resolution & ending – The last scene is my dad returning my phone me in a year's time and me not even looking at it. The personal essay finishes with me promising to go out to meet friends more in real life.

Now plan out a **climax/resolution** and **ending** for some more past exam questions. You can use characters and plots from earlier **Lessons** or create new ones.

3. Write a short story which involves a race against time to prevent a disaster. (2018)

Climax/resolution & ending – _____

_____

_____

4. Write a personal essay in which you discuss what you have already achieved in life and what you hope to achieve in the future. (2018)

Climax/resolution & ending – _____

_____

_____

5. Write a personal essay giving your views on the importance of praise and encouragement as we go through life. (2017)

Climax/resolution & ending – _____

_____

_____

6. Write a short story in which the main character goes on an exciting journey and learns some valuable lessons along the way. (2016)

Climax/resolution & ending – _____

_____

_____

 ## Time to Write

To write a **climax scene**, you need to include a mixture of **action** and **emotion**. The **action** is there because the character needs to resolve any **tension** that has been built up throughout the story. Why do you think **emotion** is a key ingredient in a **climax scene**?

Let's take the example from the 2017 exam Composition question about the importance of **praise** and **encouragement**. As it is a **personal essay**, you need to think about how much you might have changed as a person because of these two keywords. Also, because it's the **climax** of a personal essay, it is told from the **perspective** of you in the exam hall in June.

Definition

Perspective: means the point of view of the narrator or character.

Remember, for a personal essay you have to bring it back to you right at that moment sitting the Leaving Cert exam in June. Say how the experience has helped to shape the person you are now.

I think again about my Leaving Cert. After coming this far, I feel _____

_____

Without the praise of my family, I would never have been able to _____

_____

The encouragement when I was down to keep going meant that I _____

_____

_____

All that is needed now is the **ending**. Simply hint at what is to come in the future.

So I know that when I'm done here, I will praise and encourage people because _____

_____

_____

For a **short story**, your **climax scene** has to be a little bit more dramatic with a bit more **action**. For this example, we will look at the 'centre of attention' question from the 2019 paper. As it is a short story, the narrator can be anyone, so you can make up their age and where the story takes place. Remember Justin from **Lesson 26**? Now we find out if he's made it to the final:

It was the night of the final. No one would have known those months ago when Justin first arrived that _____

_____

It was just so unexpected. The lights went down and the crowd held its breath. Then he began his routine. It was _____

_____

_____

All the hard work had paid off.

Again, all you need to do next is write an **ending**. What happened after the show? Where is Justin now?

Why won't you forget that night? What happened that was so memorable? How did you feel?

That was eight years ago, now. I'll never forget it because _____

_____

_____

He is out there _____

_____

What is Justin doing now? Movies? TV? Gigs and tours?

and I am proud to have been a small part of his unexpected success.

Time to Impress

Foreshadowing

This technique was mentioned in the **Description and reveal** section of **Lesson 22** on **short story** and **personal essay** writing. It means to mention something earlier in the **composition** that is important later on.

The **climax scene** is a great place to tie up any **foreshadowing** you may have used in your writing. Look at this example to see how it's used, then complete the example afterwards.

Here is one about a letter:

Earlier in the piece:

The letter with the hospital logo on it was on the table when I walked in. My dad quickly tucked it away. He thought I hadn't see it.

Climax scene:

My mind went back to the letter. Now I knew why he had tried to hide it. He didn't want me to worry about him. I loved him for that. But now I had a chance to help him.

_____

_____

_____

Climax scene:

How did you feel after finding out that Steve was lying? The clothes aren't important; it is the **emotion** you feel at being lied to that is.

Now it all made sense. Steve had lied that night. Brian <u>had</u> been there. I felt like _____

_____

_____

Class/Homework exercise

- Look at the following descriptions and write a **climax scene** for them.
- Focus on what happens and how the **character feels** at the end of the story.

1. Jamal has worked hard to get to the top of his profession as an architect. Now he is going for a top job with the biggest firm in the country. Write the **climax scene** where he goes for the interview.

2. Sarah injured herself in the semi-final of the championship. She has been in the gym and at the physiotherapist recovering for three weeks. There are ten minutes left of the final and her coach puts her on. Write the **climax scene** where she gets the winning score.

3. Neil has sacrificed time with his friends and his family to work on his music. Now he is performing on stage in the National Concert Hall. Write the **climax scene** where he impresses the audience and how it was all worth it.

4. Fatima has talked about how she spends her free time lazing around and relaxing. Write the **climax paragraph** of her **personal essay** where she tells the reader just how important it is to relax and enjoy themselves sometimes.

- In pairs, take the following list of basic items and discuss how they could be used to show **foreshadowing** in a piece of writing.
- Then write a brief explanation of how you could use them in your story or essay.

Example for a story using a book as a foreshadowing item:

Earlier in the story the grandad could say it meant a lot to him, and then, later, the narrator could read it. This lets him get closer to his grandad.

- A key
- A necklace
- A pen
- A teddy bear
- A hairclip
- A phone
- A notification beep
- A coffee cup
- A chess piece
- A football boot
- A snow globe

 Time to Reflect

1. What is the purpose of a **climax scene**?
2. What do the words 'suspense' and 'resolution' mean?
3. Why do you need to use **action** in a **climax scene** for a short story?
4. Why is **emotion** needed in the **climax scene** for a personal essay?
5. Why do readers want an **ending** that says what happens next to the characters?
6. Why is the **climax scene** a good place to tie up any **foreshadowing** in your story?

LESSON 28: PERSONAL ESSAY – STRUCTURE AND PLANNING

Learning Objectives – By the end of this lesson you should:

- Understand what a **personal essay** is and how it's different from a **short story**
- Know what each part of the **plan** for a **personal essay** contains
- Know how to **structure** a **personal essay** and write a 100-mark Composition

 Time to Think

Personal essays are very different to short stories. A story can take place anywhere to anyone, at any time. You can use any **genre**, such as **fantasy**, **romance**, or **thriller**. Anyone can be the **narrator**.

But for a **personal essay**, *you* –sitting your Leaving Certificate exam in June – are the **narrator**. What do you think the examiner is looking for in this kind of composition?

You may feel this is a problem because you don't have enough real-life experience to answer the question. But that's okay. The you in the personal essay story is a **fictional** you. If you need to make things up or exaggerate, that's fine. They will make your essay all the better.

So think about it: what challenges are there in writing a **personal essay**? How important is it to add in your own experiences and thoughts? What opportunities do you have to tell your own story?

PCLM

P – For the **personal essay**, you need to understand that it must be from *your* **perspective**. The examiner is looking for your take on the question. Of course, you include stories in the essay, but it can't read like a short story.

C – The **structure** needs to be **clear and coherent**. Make sure to plan your answer in advance.

Exploring the structure of a personal essay

When you are writing a personal essay, if you follow this **7-step structure** your essay will have **coherence**. Each step is vital in creating the essay.

1. **Theme** – Explore the **themes** in the question.

2. **Setting** – Describe **your world** to the reader. Keep the **themes** in mind.

3. **Character creation** – For a personal essay, *you* are the central character, so describe yourself. You only really have space for one other main character, either an **antagonist** or a **sidekick/friend**.

4. **Topic 1 (Positive)** – Begin your essay by speaking about the question keywords in a positive way. Explain your examples, and how they affect you as a person.

5. **Topic 2 (Negative)** – Then talk about how the question has affected you negatively. Discuss any difficulties you've had, and how you can overcome them.

6. **Topic 3 (Hopeful)** – Now explain how you are going to tackle a new thing using what you've learned from experiences in your life so far.

> Each topic should take around three paragraphs, or roughly 200 words, to explore.

7. **Climax and resolution** – Finally, you just wrap up your personal essay. Say how your experiences have shaped you as a person, and how you are going to use them to grow in the future.

We will work on a sample answer on a question from the 2016 exam using this **structure**.

> **Choose any two themes and plan out your experience of them.**
>
> Write a (personal essay) about your own experience of (any two) of the following: kindness, patience, generosity, tolerance, and forgiveness.

The general **plan** for this question could be:

1: *Kindness – How it was shown to me after I moved schools. How Katie became my new best friend.*

2: *Forgiveness – I find it hard to forgive. I've been burned too many times.*

3: *Kindness – How I'm trying to give back to my new area, and to the people who were so kind to me, by volunteering my time.*

Read the following seven sample sections and see how they combine into one **coherent** answer. The essay is in the **first person** ('I') as all **personal essays** should be.

As you read each step, discuss the questions given in groups or pairs.

1. Theme

Our lives today are really busy. Hectic isn't the word. We race from thing to thing without ever thinking about what we are doing. It seems like it's just instinct half the time. If we are kind, it's almost like a reaction. We don't think, we just are. Whether we show forgiveness or not is the same. I am eighteen now, and I've gone through a lot. Here is how it's shaped me, for better and for worse.

(78 words)

Why is it important to talk about the **themes** you've chosen? How is this paragraph personal? Circle the parts in the paragraph where you can see the **themes**.

2. Setting

To be honest, being a teenager in the 2020s is tough. I know every generation has probably said that, but they were right as well. The unnecessary dramas we face is a killer on our health, physically and mentally. The world of a young adult is harsh and unforgiving. We don't just have a private life in our homes and clubs: we have a public one, lived out on people's phone screens. That's a world only celebrities had in years gone by. But for us, this is normal.

There are many positives to social media, but also many negatives. What do you think this image is trying to say?

(88 words)

What is the **setting** described? Is it a harsh world? Realistic? Does it link to the **themes**?

3. Character creation

Appearance

Well, it's normal for me and my friends, anyway. I like dressing up and going out. I like the way I feel when I've spent that time on <u>me</u>. *People might try to say I love myself; that I'm vain, but I just think it's important to feel good. And for me, feeling good starts with looking good. That's where my confidence comes from. But don't get me wrong, I love a good night in front of the TV as much as the next person.*

(85 words)

Personality

I think people say I'm quite a (kind) person. That's why I chose that word from the list. I'd do anything for my friends and family, and I think they'd do the same for me. Only last week I can remember being a shoulder to cry on for a good friend of mine, Katie. You just don't know what people are going through. But the other thing – (forgiveness) – that's something that doesn't come naturally. I've been burned too many times.

(80 words)

Why is it important to give a sense of **personality** in your essay? How does this help the reader? Why are the circled words mentioned?

4. Topic 1 (Positive) – Kindness

So what is my experience of kindness? Looking at this honestly, I don't think I experienced much of this when I was younger. I remember in my last school when girls would talk behind my back, and the lads would spread rumours about me. Kindness wasn't really in their vocabulary. It's hard living in a world without kindness for eight hours a day. I can only be thankful for my family who were always there for me.

As luck would have it, it was my family who got me out of that mess. My da got a new job, and we had to move. I was terrified of starting in a new school, especially after what happened the last time, but Katie showed me that kindness can be in places you don't expect to see it. She saw I was new, introduced herself on the morning of day one, and helped me get used to everything from timetables to clubs.

I really can't overstate how much that meant to me. The kindness she showed, especially when she didn't have to, really embodies the wonderful person she is. It is pretty inspiring and something that I want to keep going. About a year later, a new guy started, and the first thing I did was say hello to him. Those little acts of kindness mean a lot and stay with people.

(230 words over three paragraphs)

A scene from the film Mean Girls, *which shows how high school politics can work.*

What was the narrator like before she experienced kindness? What was the kindness she received and how did it affect her? How did the paragraphs show character development?

5. Topic 2 (Negative) – Forgiveness

But if someone ever does something to me, I find it so hard to forgive. I think it all goes back to my old school. I tried really hard to fit in, but it just wasn't happening for me. If I wore the right clothes, it was a week too late. If I watched the latest show everyone was talking about, no one listened to what I had to say about it. Generally, no one cared about how much I tried.

Well, Amelia did. Or, at least, she seemed to. We were friends all the way up from Baby Infants to Third Year. Inseparable, my ma used to say. It was handy because Amelia lived next door, and we would spend most of our waking hours together. She was always there for me when the popular kids shot me down. And I was there for her when she didn't get picked for the team she so desperately wanted to be a part of.

Then there was an opening at the popular kids' table. I swear it was like an American high school movie. One kid moved away, and Amelia jumped into her seat before it was cold. She never looked back. As a popular kid, she didn't need me anymore. I knocked for her and sent her a text a few times afterwards. Just silence. She texted me a few weeks ago saying sorry for how she'd treated me. I still haven't replied. Yet, anyway. It's still a bit too much. I'd rather fill my life with positivity.

(258 words over 3 paragraphs)

What was the narrator's first experience with Amelia? Was it positive? What did Amelia do that the narrator found so hard to forgive? How did this experience shape her personally?

Many people volunteer in different ways. Do you know anyone who volunteers their time with a community group or charity?

6. Topic 3 (Hopeful) – Kindness

This just brings me back to the idea of kindness I was talking about earlier. It's so important to me for people to just be nice to each other and help each other out. Katie has been volunteering at this animal shelter recently. She loves it. Like all volunteering jobs, you do it <u>because</u> you love it, and she does. Now, animals are not for me. Put a cat hair ten metres from my nose, and I'll be sneezing for a week. But I'm showing kindness in a different way.

My nanny is in a care home at the moment. She's elderly and can't really remember who I am, but I still go to down to see her at least three times a week. I'm lucky that it's only a nice twenty-minute stroll away. It's tough seeing her like that, but I think my nanny really appreciates the visits. Just one look around at some of the other ladies tells you that not everyone gets shown that kindness. Her locker is full of flowers and cards. Her neighbour's is as barren as a desert.

I try to make it my business to chat with everyone I can down there. I know from my experience with Amelia and Katie that even tiny acts of kindness, like a smile or a quick few words about Fair City, can make some poor old woman's day (as bleak as that can sound to young ears). I don't think my nanny minds sharing my company too much when I'm down there. She's a kind soul herself.

(261 words over three paragraphs)

How was the narrator inspired to show kindness? How does she show her grandmother and the other elderly women kindness? Why does she do it?

7. Climax and resolution

Which brings me back to the question itself: my experience of kindness and forgiveness. What has it taught me? Well, it's taught me to be a better person. We can only really grow as people when we've gone through something. Anyone can tell us what hurt and forgiveness are, what hate and kindness feel like, but unless we go through them, live them, then their words are just that – words. My experiences have shaped me into the kind person I am today. Maybe I'll send Amelia a text when I get out of the exam.

(95 words) (Total: 1,175 words)

How has the narrator summed up her experience of the **themes**? Why do you think she mentioned the exam at the end?

Question analysis

For a personal essay, you must figure out the **theme** in the question before you start writing. Once you have this done, you can begin to **plan** your answer. All the important **personal essay** writing skills you need are explored in **Lessons 21 to 27** of this workbook.

The following are all past exam questions. Write down a brief description of what the themes for each personal essay could be about. Try to think of three topics for each essay:

> Write a personal essay in which you discuss at least three aspects of life that are considered unremarkable in 2019 that you think may appear strange or remarkable to people in the future. (2019)

1. *Living our lives on social media. They might think it's mad that we put everything on the Internet.*

2. *Driving everywhere. In the future, I think they would have more eco-friendly ways to get around.*

3. *Racism. As people keep moving from place to place, and we become more global, I hope people will think racism was a strange thing.*

> Write a personal essay in which you discuss what you think your life would be like if you were unable to use any form of social media for a whole year. (2019)

1. *I would get out more and be more active.*

2. _____

3. _____

4. _____

> Think of another impact of not being able to use social media for a year. Try to make it a more hopeful one.

> Write a personal essay in which you discuss the importance of at least three of the following in your life: family, friends, health, school, fun, and work. (2018)

1. Family – They support me and care for me even when it might seem they are putting pressure on me, or stop me from doing what I want.

2. _____
   _____

3. _____
   _____

Pick any two of the other items on the list and say how important they are to you.

> Write a personal essay in which you discuss what you have already achieved in life and what you hope to achieve in the future. (2018)

1. _____

2. _____

3. _____

> Write a personal essay giving your views on the importance of praise and encouragement as we go through life. (2017)

1. _____

2. _____

3. _____

Time to Write

Now that you have a good idea as to how the **7-step structure** works, and you've seen samples of it, you can plan an answer yourself. Look at this question from the 2018 exam paper:

> Write a personal essay in which you discuss what you have already achieved in life and what you hope to achieve in the future. (2018)

1. **Theme:** _____
   _____
   _____

Read the question and circle the themes. How are they going to be important in your story?

2. Setting: _____

_____

_____

> The question is a **personal essay**, so create a world you are familiar with. Describe your home, your area, your school, or any place that makes your setting more realistic and rounded.

3. Characters:

   (a) Protagonist: _____

   _____

   _____

   _____

   > You are the **protagonist** in the story. Describe the kind of person you are, but link your description to the themes in the question. Are you a person who is driven to succeed? Or do you find it difficult to overcome failure? Focus on both your appearance and personality.

   (b) Antagonist: _____

   _____

   _____

   _____

   > Is there a person who continually gets in your way? Describe them. Is there a feeling, like not thinking you're good enough or that you're too shy, that stops you achieving?

   (c) Friend/sidekick: _____

   _____

   _____

   _____

   > Describe the person that helps you through the tough times. This could be a friend, family member, teacher, whoever.

4. Topic 1 (Positive): _____

_____

_____

_____

> Talk about one of your successes that came easily enough. What did you want to achieve? What did you have to do to achieve it? What stood in your way and what did you have to do to overcome it?

5. Topic 2 (Negative): _____

_____

_____

_____

> What did you achieve that came after a struggle? How did you feel when things weren't going well? What was holding you back? What helped you finally overcome the hard times and succeed?

6. Topic 3 (Hopeful): _____

_____

_____

_____

> What is the big thing you hope to achieve in the future? What do you need to do to get this? What possible things will you need to overcome? How hopeful are you that you'll accomplish this?

7. Climax and resolution: _____

_____

_____

> How much do you think you have grown over the last few years from what you've achieved in life so far? How **positive** do you feel about the future?

 ## Time to Finish

You've planned your answer and written some sample paragraphs; now it's time to write your answer out in full on a separate page.

Class/Homework exercise

- Look at the following **themes** that weren't used in the sample answer.
- Think about how you feel about each **theme**.
- Think of a brief story (**anecdote**) to go along with each one.
- Now write a sample **topic** like the topics in the sample.

1. Patience
2. Generosity
3. Tolerance

 ## Time to Reflect

1. What is a **personal essay**?

2. How is it different to a **short story**?

3. Is it in the **first person** or **third person perspective**? Why?

4. List the stages in the **7-step structure**. Why should you discuss **theme** and create a **setting** at the start of your essay?

5. How many paragraphs of narrative, roughly, should you have for each **topic**? (This is just a guide. If you use dialogue, then there may be more paragraphs.)

6. What does the **climax** do at the end of your **personal essay**?

Composing

Learning Objectives – By the end of this lesson you should:

- Know the **structure** of a **short story**
- Understand how each section works and why it's needed for **coherence**
- Be able to plan a **short story** and write a 100-mark **composition**

 Time to Think

The writer of the *Game of Thrones* books, George R.R. Martin, has said that some writers are like **gardeners** who plant seeds (ideas) and see where they go. But this way of writing takes a lot of time, practise, and editing, as you have no idea where the story will go. For the Leaving Certificate you don't have the time to do this. You have to be more like an **architect**. As Martin says:

> The architects plan everything ahead of time, like an architect building a house. They have the whole thing designed and blueprinted out before they even nail the first board up.

Source: *The Guardian*, 'Getting More from George R.R. Martin' by Alison Flood

How, according to Martin, is an architect similar to a writer?

Do you think it's important to plan your story out in advance before you start writing?

What would happen if you just started writing without thinking it through in advance?

Writing a **short story** can be difficult for students. At Junior Cycle, stories are usually quite short. For Leaving Certificate, it is completely different. This lesson is here to show you how to **structure and plan** a **short story**. Once you know the structure and know how to plan your answer, you will find short stories much easier to write.

PCLM

P – For a **short story**, you need to understand that the question gives you room to write in an exciting and imaginative way. You also need to make sure that the question **keywords** are properly used in your story.

C – **Coherence** is another word for **structure**. Having a clear and well-put-together short story will mean that your **coherence** mark will be high.

Exploring the structure of a short story

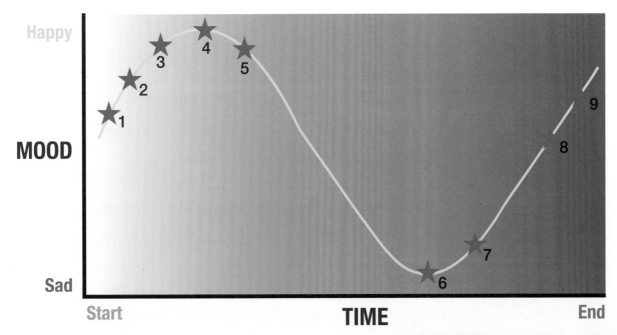

When you are writing a short story, there is an easy-to-follow **9-point plan** to structure it that works really well. Let's use a film that is often on the Leaving Certificate course – *Les Misérables* – to show examples for each section.

On the barricade: 'Do You Hear the People Sing?' from Les Misérables.

1. Theme – Explore the theme that is in the question.

Jean Valjean is seen in prison clothes dragging a boat into dry dock. We can clearly see how miserable his life is. This links with the title of the film. It shows the misery of his life and how he must look for redemption.

2. Setting – Create a world for your character to live in.

The setting is 19th-century France as Javert's clothing and the old-fashioned buildings show quickly. Setting a scene in the church early in the story sets up the theme of Jean Valjean's redemption later on.

3. Character creation – Bring your character to life by describing by their **appearance** and **personality**.

We see Jean Valjean in jail. We learn that he is there for stealing a loaf of bread to feed his starving nephew. This makes us feel a connection with him.

4. High point – Describe how everything is **going great** for your character before the bad thing happens.

Valjean has turned his life around after being saved by a priest. He now runs a factory and is the town's mayor.

5. Action – Create an **action scene** where your character's world is turned upside down.

Valjean must break his parole to get to this high point in his life. The police think they recognise him, and Valjean must consider running away.

6. Low point – Describe your character at their **lowest emotional point** before they turn it around.

A woman who Valjean wrongly fired from his factory dies after living on the streets, and he blames himself.

7. Turning point – Explain what happens to your character that **motivates** them **to succeed** in the final part of your story.

Valjean saves the dead woman's child and brings her up after making her mother a promise on her deathbed. They leave the town for a new life.

8. Climax and resolution – The part of your story where the **plot** is **resolved**.

Valjean then saves his adopted daughter's fiancé during a rebellion. This gives him the redemption he seeks. He dies soon afterwards, exhausted but happy that his daughter and her true love are safe.

9. Ending – Hint at what will happen to the characters after the story.

The film ends on a positive note with all the dead characters singing a reprise of 'Do You Hear the People Sing?' on a huge barricade, possibly showing how their sacrifice might still mean something.

Now we will work through a sample answer for a question from the 2016 paper:

> Write a short story in which the main character goes on an (exciting journey) and learns some (valuable lessons) along the way. (2016)

> There are two **themes** mentioned in the question: **journeys** and **valuable lessons.**

The general plot line could be:

Abdul is kid who has it all and doesn't really care about anyone else. He thinks he's on a free holiday to Morocco, but, in reality, he's there to help build a school. By doing this, he learns to appreciate what he has and to be nicer to others.

Read the **nine sample sections** and watch how they become one **coherent short story**. This example is in the **third person** (he/she/they), but short stories can also be in the **first person** (I). As you read each part, discuss the questions given in groups or pairs.

1. Theme:

What does it mean to 'learn your lesson'? Abdul had heard this phrase loads of times. 'He's a spoilt kid; he should be taught a lesson' or 'Someone should teach him some respect.' But it never really bothered him. Who were they to say anything about him? He acted the way he wanted and nothing could change that. And then going to Morocco happened, and his world turned upside down.

(70 words)

Why is it important to talk about the **themes** at the **start** of your story?

Circle where the **themes** are mentioned in the above paragraph.

2. Setting:

Abdul's family came to Ireland from there twenty years ago. He had never even been to the place. All he knew was some estate out in the suburbs where the cars were nice, the clothes were new, and graffiti didn't exist. Good living was his goal in life. He had his own large room and every piece of tech that a person could need. Yes, he was wealthy, and he wasn't going to apologise for it.

(76 words)

Why is it important to create a realistic and well-described world for your characters to live in? What **setting** is described here?

3. Character creation:

Personality

Well, his parents were wealthy, anyway. Abdul knew he got the best of things because his parents felt that they had nothing growing up. So he should have everything now. He remembered his dad telling him about when they arrived in Ireland. They had a suitcase and nothing else. They told him they worked their asses off to get to the top. Abdul just smiled his cheeky smile and took their money. His dad tutted and said his lesson was coming.

(81 words)

Appearance

But what lesson? He was a popular seventeen-year-old kid who didn't have to worry about a thing. People just flocked to him. His latest Balenciaga runners caused envy with every step, and his perfect smile entranced his friends and enemies alike. No one could ever say Abdul wasn't the most popular kid in the school. But the kids he laughed at every day could describe him as the least-liked.

(69 words)

What is Abdul like? Why do you think is it important to flesh out your character early in the story? Where is there an element of **foreshadowing** in the first paragraph?

4. High point:

All in all, his life was brilliant. Not a day would go by when he wouldn't laugh at how so many in his year would go around in hand-me-down jackets and wear cheap shoes. He was top of the mountain in school. He hadn't a care in the world. He was so proud of the reputation he'd built himself. But as they say, pride comes before a fall, and Abdul's fall had a pretty big drop.

(76 words)

Why do you think you should show your character to be very happy before disaster happens?

5. Action:

On the Friday before the Easter break, Abdul's dad came into room. His face told Abdul that he was in trouble, but he just grinned as this usually worked to get him out of it. But no. Not this time.

An image of the Moroccan city, Marrakech.

'Abdul, we're off on a journey to Morocco in the morning. No arguments.' His father's voice was low and stern, and he held a leaflet in his hand.

'Grand! I'll pack the shorts, so,' Abdul replied coolly. His dad dropped the leaflet on his locker, but Abdul just left it there. His head was full of resorts and golden beaches.

Twenty-four hours later, he realised just how wrong he was. They were staying with his uncle, and Abdul was lugging heavy wheelbarrows full of thick cement up dirt hills towards a building site. He didn't think he had ever been as angry.

'To hell with this!' Abdul shouted after the tenth trip sent wet cement over his new runners. He had stumbled after hitting a rock trying to avoid some little kid. He tipped the barrow on its side and stormed off. His dad saw him and shouted for Abdul to come back. But he just kept going, even though he heard the disappointment in his father's voice.

(208 words over 5 paragraphs)

For a reader, why should there be **action** in a story? What is the **action** here? Do Abdul's actions seem in character (what we would expect him to do)?

6. Low point:

Abdul found a space behind a tool shed and sat down sadly. He wasn't going back to his uncle's house as he knew his dad would be there looking for him. He didn't want to see his father's judging face. He was so angry with his dad. Why had he brought him there? He didn't want to waste his precious holidays on a bloody building site. His eyes were burning with tears at the injustice of it all.

(78 words)

Why should your character feel really bad at this point of the story? How is Abdul feeling?

7. Turning point:

Then, a little kid appeared. It was the same one who'd made him spill the wet cement earlier. She just looked at him and dropped a piece of paper at his feet. 'Thanks,' she said, and walked away.

Abdul looked down and realised the paper was the same leaflet his dad had left on his locker. There was a building on the front with kids in uniforms holding books. <u>That's</u> why he was there. The community was building a school, and his dad wanted to give something back to the place that raised him. All of a sudden, Abdul didn't think shame was a strong enough a word for how he felt.

(112 words over two paragraphs)

Why would a character need **inspiration** to turn it around? What inspires Abdul?

8. Climax and resolution:

Abdul got up immediately and ran back to the site. He found his dad and hugged him so tight that he was sure he heard ribs crack.

Abdul saw the stunned look on his father's face. Then his dad hugged him back. He could see by Abdul's face and the leaflet in his hand that he was sorry and wanted to keep going.

Which is what Abdul did. Not once over the next two weeks did he complain. He was a new man. The building was nearly finished by the time they left. But just before heading for the airport, Abdul found that little kid again and said, 'Thanks,' back. She'd never fully know the lesson she taught him that day.

(121 words over three paragraphs)

Why does a story need an **action scene** near the end? How is the **plot resolved**?

How can we see **character development**?

9. Ending:

So the excitement wasn't actually from the holiday of a lifetime. It was from a different kind of journey: one of giving back and getting closer to his dad. The excitement was there when they were building the school, and again when they saw the pictures of it finished two months later. His dad was right when he said Abdul needed to learn his lesson. He just didn't think he'd have to go to a school in Morocco to do so.

(81 words) (Total: 972 words.)

Why do you think the reader wants to know what happens to characters after the story is over? Circle the **question keywords** in the paragraph. Why are they mentioned?

Question analysis

For a **short story**, one of the most important things to do once you see the question is to figure out the **theme**. Once you have this done, you can begin to **structure** your answer. All the important story-writing skills you need are explored in **Lessons 21 to 27** of this workbook.

For the following past exam questions, circle the **theme** and then write down a brief description of what the **storyline** could be:

> Write a short story in which a group of (childhood friends) form what becomes a world-famous band but live to [regret] their [success.] (2019)

We start the band in school. We have a hit song. Then fame gets to the lead singer's head. They go solo but fail, regretting how big-headed they were. The band reunites at the end, and they go back to being friends.

Write a short story about a character whose (determination) to be the centre of (attention) has unexpected consequences. (2019)

The class clown is always very funny. On a school trip, Simon Cowell notices him and invites him onto Britain's Got Talent.

**What happens next?
Does he succeed?
Finish the plan.**

Write a short story in which confusion arises because the two central characters, brothers or sisters, are identical twins. Identical twins are twins who look exactly alike. (2018)

Sarah and Lara are twins but complete opposites. Sarah is great at sport and Lara isn't. Sarah is due to get a scholarship to an American college. Then she hurts her leg in the lead-up to the final.

**What happens next? What
does Lara do to help Sarah?
Does it work?**

Write a short story which features a character who gets into trouble because of his or her sense of humour. (2017)

Write a short story in which a family comes to regret adopting a robot. (2017)

 **Time to Write**

So now it's time to plan your own **short story**. What are the most important things to think of before you start writing? Why is it so important to have your **storyline** prepared in advance?

Write a short story which involves **a race against time to prevent a disaster.**

1. Theme: _____

_____

_____

> Read the question and circle the **themes**. How are they going to be important in your story?

2. Setting: _____

_____

_____

> The question is about a 'disaster'. Where might the disaster take place? What is the place like now? How will it change if the disaster isn't prevented?

3. Characters:

(a) Protagonist: _____

_____

_____

> Who is the **main character** who will try to prevent the disaster? Briefly describe them. Which **perspective** is the story in: **first person** or **third person**?

(b) Antagonist: _____

_____

_____

> What is causing the disaster? Is it a natural thing like an earthquake? Or is it a person? Describe the event or the person.

(c) Friend/sidekick: _____

_____

> Who is the person that helps the protagonist along the way? Will they argue? How will they get back together?

4. High point: _____

_____

_____

_____

> Describe how good life was before the disaster.

5. Action: _____

_____

_____

_____

> What happens to begin the race against time to prevent the disaster?

Composing

6. Low point: _____

_____

How does the protagonist **feel** when they think they can't prevent it?

_____

7. Turning point: _____

_____

What turns it around for them?

_____

8. Climax and resolution: _____

_____

How do they prevent the disaster? How does the protagonist feel after succeeding?

_____

9. Ending: _____

_____

What happens after the story finishes?

_____

 ## Time to Finish

With your answer planned and some sample paragraphs written, it's time to write your answer in full on a separate page.

Class/Homework exercise

- Choose a film you have watched or a text you have studied in class.

- Write a sentence about when the following parts happened in the storyline:

1. Theme	**4.** High point	**7.** Turning point
2. Setting	**5.** Action	**8.** Climax
3. Character creation	**6.** Low point	**9.** Ending

 ## Time to Reflect

1. Why is it important to plan a **short story** in advance?

2. What are you looking for in a **short story** question to help you answer it?

3. What does '**resolution**' mean?

4. Name all of the sections in the **9-point plan**, and explain the importance of each section.

5. Why will your **coherence** mark be higher if your **short story** follows the plan?

6. Why is **character development** important in your story? What does it add to it?

LESSON 30: SPEECH – STRUCTURE AND PLANNING

Learning Objectives – By the end of this lesson you should:

- Know what a **speech** is and how it differs from a **talk**
- Know different techniques that make a speech more **interactive** and **engaging**
- Be able to plan and successfully write an answer to a 100-mark question

 ## Time to Think

What makes a **speech** different to a **talk**?

That is a key question that students must understand when they write a **speech**. One of the main differences is **tone (or register)**. For a **talk**, the **register** can be a lot less formal and a lot more friendly. For a **speech**, you must look at the topic seriously, even if you are using humour. The other difference is length. The **speech** question is worth 100 marks, so you will need more planning before you write it.

So what is a **speech** designed to do? Think about when you might deliver one. In past exams, students have been asked to imagine they are speaking in front of the United Nations, their classmates, and their teachers. In another year, they were asked to pretend they were a member of the Irish Society for the Prevention of Cruelty to Animals. How does each **audience** affect the **register**? In each case, students were asked to relate information to people in a **clear**, **informative**, and **persuasive** way.

Here is an example from one of the most famous speeches of all time, the 'I have a dream' speech by Reverend Dr Martin Luther King Jr.

'I have a dream that my four little children will one day live in a nation where they will not be judged by the color of their skin but by the content of their character.'

What makes Dr King's words so powerful? What **tone** does he take? Who do you think he is speaking to? Just the crowd that's there, or to anyone who will ever hear or read the words? Your **speech** doesn't have to be as important as his, but it must be **honest** and **persuasive**.

PCLM

P – You must understand that your **speech** is designed to be spoken and received by the **audience**. It has to move them **emotionally** as well as make them **think**.

L – The language of **persuasion**, **information**, and **argument** are key here, as is the fact that you must write knowing that you are being listened to by a group of people.

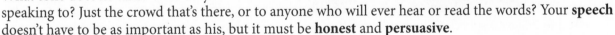

Composing

Exploring a speech

Students at Leaving Certificate level will have done presentations before. At Junior Cycle you would have done them in several subjects. A presentation, though, is mainly about delivering information. What does a speech do that's different? Look at the following sample paragraph from the 2019 exam question about the 'responsibilities facing humanity' as we explore space and try to figure this out. The speech is delivered to the UN:

The floor of the UN headquarters in New York during a debate.

We students see the familiar world around us as one in crisis. As we look into the skies and see strange worlds like Mars and the Moon, that for the first time look like places we can live on, we must know our responsibilities. We have done so much damage to our home planet that we must make sure we don't continue it in space. Everyone here today is a decision-maker in your own country. Make sure the decisions you make are wise ones.

(84 words)

1. How is space mentioned in the paragraph? _____
   _____

2. What **register** is used? Is it the correct **tone** to use to address the UN?_____
   _____

3. How does the speaker refer to the **audience**? How do we know it is being spoken out loud?
   _____
   _____

Question analysis

Now look at the following question from the 2017 paper. Often, the **speech** questions are quite long, so make sure to read them properly and analyse them fully.

> Imagine that you have been selected as the Student of the Year in your school and have been asked to deliver a speech to the staff and students at a school assembly. The topic for your speech is 'My School Days'. Write the speech, which may be serious or humorous or both, that you would deliver.

1. Who is the **audience**?_____
   _____

2. Explain how you would speak to this kind of **audience**. _____
   _____

3. Circle the **title** of the speech you have to give.

4. Because the question is very broad, this can make **planning** difficult. Why do you think that is?

_____

_____

Let's look at **structure** and **planning**. It will be a long answer, and you will need to think about your **ideas** before you start writing. You must include:

Structure – Speech

An introduction

- An engaging opening line to grab the **audience**'s attention.

- Say who you are and why you are there to speak.

- Outline (but not explain) what you are going to speak about.

The main body of the answer

- **Ten to 12** planned IRE paragraphs of about **70 to 80** words each.

- You can write individual paragraphs that deal with one point.

- Or you can **develop a point** over two or three paragraphs.

- You must **link** them to add to your **coherence** mark.

A conclusion

- **Recap** all of the **main points** made.

- Remind the **audience** who you are and why you are there to speak.

- Finish with a **statement** that makes the **audience** remember you.

Now we can work on **planning** an answer. One hundred marks is a lot, and the question only gives you one thing to talk about: 'my school days'. This means that it is up to you to think of other headings to work on. Here are some samples with space for you to fill in some others yourself:

1. Getting used to school in 1st Year.

2. Playing sport.

3. Making friends for life.

4. Performing in the school play.

5. _____

6. _____

7. _____

8. _____

Let's now take one of the headings and **brainstorm** a few things we could include in the **speech**:

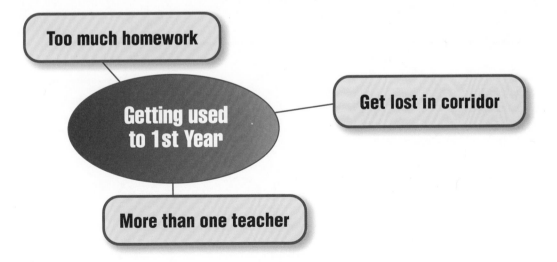

Once you have this done for **one topic**, then you can do it for **three more**. This gives you lots to talk about in your speech.

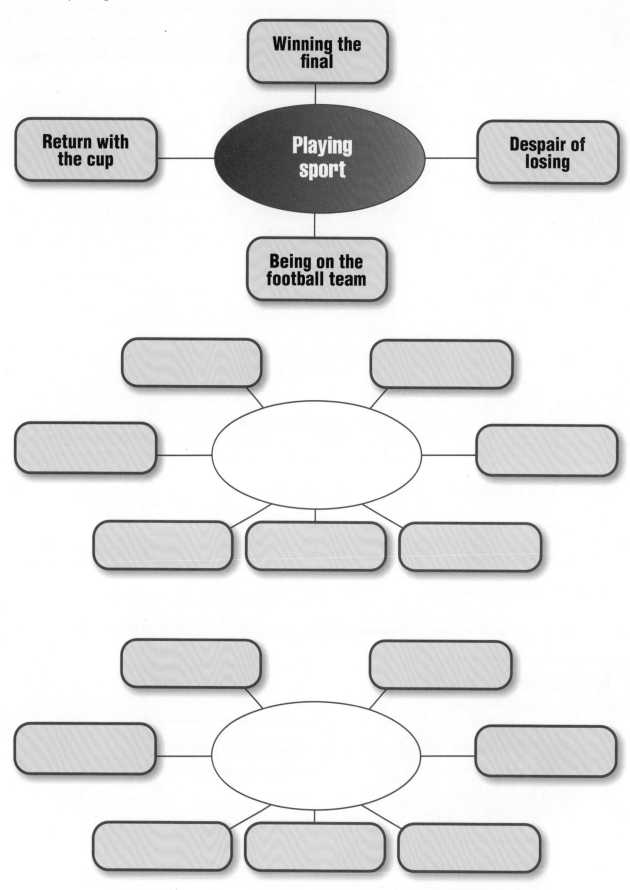

Time to Write

Now that the planning is completed, we can start to write out the answer. The first part is the **introduction**. Finish the sample below with help from the prompts:

> **How does it feel to give the speech and win the award?**

Here we are today, classmates and teachers. It feels _____

_____

_____

I am Ally Owens, and I am so proud to _____

_____

I don't want to keep you long, but this place means a lot to me. I want to tell you about

_____

_____

> **In just one sentence, say why you are there.**

> **In a bit more detail, say what you will be speaking about.**

For each of the **main body** paragraphs, you should follow the **IRE** approach. There is a sample above, but here's one to complete. This is the **first of two paragraphs** about the **idea** of 'getting used to school in 1st Year'. In the first, you set up and explain the point, and in the second, you go into a lot more detail.

Imagine all of the students listening to your speech. It is vital to keep them interested.

> **List off some of your ideas from the brainstorm.**

Seeing as this is our last day in school, I want to start by talking about our first all those years ago. Starting in 1st Year was tough: _____

_____

But the thing I found the hardest was the movement between classes because _____

_____

_____

> **What was so hard about moving between classes? Getting lost? Bumped by 6th Years?**

One you've opened up your **idea**, it's then time to go into a lot more detail. You can do this by:

- Telling an anecdote (brief story to prove your point)
- Giving a statistic
- Quoting someone with experience
- Showing research

Complete the next paragraph, which uses some of these techniques.

> Before I came up on stage, I asked my fellow 6th Years, 'Who felt comfortable in their first month of school?' Their response made me smile.
> _____
> _____

This is **research**. What did you find out by talking to your fellow students?

> A recent study by the Irish Union of Secondary Students about pupils starting post-primary school found that _____
> _____
> _____

Make up a believable statistic. What percentage of students around the country felt comfortable in their first month of school? 0%? 50%? 100%?

> This tells me that it wasn't just tough for me, it was _____
> _____
> _____

What does this tell you? Were you on your own?

> I don't think I would have been able to survive if it wasn't for being on the football team.

Finally, you will need a **conclusion** where you sum up your **ideas** and leave the **audience** with something to think about. Don't forget to refer to the question.

Quickly **recap** some of the points you made.

> So what were my school days like? Well, they had _____
> _____
>
> But I wouldn't change them for the world. As Student of the Year, I'd like thank all students and staff for my wonderful years here. Let me just finish by saying
> _____
> _____
> _____

Leave the **audience** with a **question** or a **statement** to think about.

 Time to Finish

With your answer planned and some sample paragraphs done, it's now time to complete your answer on a separate page.

Time to Impress

A **speech** is an interactive experience. It is hard to imagine someone speaking for 1,200 words without any kind of **audience** interaction. So, it's up to you be creative in adding this **interaction** into your speech. You also need to show **research**. A **speech** should look like a lot of time and effort has gone into writing it. Here are two **ideas** as to how to improve the content of your speech:

As a stand-up comedian, Jimmy Carr would have to put up with heckles and interruptions.

Heckle (someone calling out from the audience):

Paul just shouted at me, 'What about the school trips?'
Well, Paul, thanks for the interruption, and you're right!
They made 1st Year a lot more fun because ...

How does this make your speech look more **realistic**? Have you ever had someone shout at you when you were speaking to try and distract you? What was your reaction?

Stats and quotes

Chances are, you won't know stats and quotes about the topic your speech is on. But the question is there to see how well you can write a speech, not if you have done research. So, feel free to make them up, **once they are believable**.

> Make up a name.

> Think of a subject or a department. If the speech is about travel, it will be Geography. If it is about social media, it will be Computers. What department should go in this sample if it is about school and students?

In a recent study by Dr _____ of the _____ department of _____, it was found that _____ per cent of people joined a club or society in school.

> Choose a university or a college.

> Write down a number between 0 and 100, but make sure it looks reasonable.

Tip For Success

Rebuttal

When writing a speech, you need to consider what the opposition will say back to you. Even the best politicians and companies do this as they need to figure out the holes in their own policies and products so that they're able to defend them. Whatever points you make in your speech, always refer to the **counter-argument** and prove them wrong.

If you're talking to the UN about the responsibilities we humans have as we explore space, feel free to talk about the people who say we should look after Earth first before spending billions on rockets. They might have a valid point, but you must try to prove them wrong. You could counter by saying exploring space has improved technologies on Earth, so the investment is worth it. Whatever point you're making, just make sure to **rebut the opposition** to enhance your **purpose** mark.

Composing

Class/Homework exercise

- Read and analyse the following questions.
- Then plan out your answers.
- Finally, write full 100-mark answers.

1. Imagine you're representing Ireland at a United Nations conference on the future. Write a speech, to be delivered at the conference, in which you discuss both the opportunities and responsibilities facing humanity as we explore space and planets beyond Earth. (2019)

2. Write a speech, to be delivered to your classmates, in which you outline the impact, both positive and negative, that technology has on your life. Your speech can be serious or amusing or both. (2018)

3. Write a speech, to be delivered to your class, in which you talk about at least one occasion in your life when you were glad you persevered with something. (2016)

4. Imagine you are a representative of the Irish Society for the Prevention of Cruelty to Animals (ISPCA). Write a speech, to be delivered in schools, in which you explain the practicalities and responsibilities involved in keeping a pet and encourage the students in your audience to treat animals with respect. (2015)

 Time to Reflect

1. What is the difference between a **speech** and a **talk**?

2. Why is it important to know who the **audience** is before you start writing the speech?

3. How should you **plan out** your speech? A **talk** will be 50 marks and a **speech** 100 marks. How does this affect your plan?

4. Each section of your answer will have at least two paragraphs. Why is that? What is the importance of the second paragraph?

5. Why should you include **audience** interaction in your speech?

6. Why should you include **facts and stats** in your speech?

LESSON 31: ARTICLE – STRUCTURE AND PLANNING

Learning Objectives – By the end of this lesson you should:

- Understand what more is needed for a 100-mark **article** question
- Be able to write an **investigation** paragraph
- Be able to plan and answer a 100-mark **composition** question

 Time to Think

Back in **Lesson 10**, we looked at how to write an **article** that is worth 50 marks. Before doing this lesson, it is recommended that you look over the **structure** of that **article** and do a little revision of that lesson.

So what more is needed to turn a 50-mark answer into a 100-mark one? Put simply, you need will need more **content.** What the examiner expects from you for 100 marks is a lot more than what they expect from you for 50 marks, but the **article structure** will be very similar: it will have an **introduction**, **main body** paragraphs, and a **conclusion.**

The big difference will be in the **main body**. Instead of your points being one paragraph, **your ideas** will be developed over **two to three paragraphs**. You will see how this works in the **planning** section below.

Tip For Success

Register and tone

Register and **tone** have been mentioned throughout this book, but it is important to remind you that they are key aspects of **purpose** in the exam marking scheme. Once you work out the **audience** (who you're speaking to), you can figure out the **register** (the correct way to speak to them).

This then lets you know the **tone** (how you speak or write the words). It can be split into three broad categories:

Formal – Keep your words very businesslike and professional. Never use slang or words like 'gonna'.

Semi-formal – The situation will be serious, like a talk, but the people will be friendly and maybe even your peers (people on the same level as you, like classmates or work colleagues). Here you can add in some humour as you make your serious point.

Informal – You will probably be speaking to someone you know very well in a personal setting or about a topic that isn't serious. You can use slang and humour in this setting.

PCLM

P – As it is an **article**, it is important to include **investigation**. This improves the level of depth in your answer.

C – It is vital to **plan** out your answer if you decide to do the 100-mark Composition question. Carefully map out what you are going to talk about before you start writing.

Exploring an article

In **Lesson 10** (page 49), you analysed the following paragraph. Look back at your answers in the earlier lesson to refresh your memory.

Lots of my friends ask me what I get from volunteering with my local football club. They know I give up two weeknights training the under 10s and most of my Saturday for their match. But let me tell you, to see the delight in the kids' faces as they play ball, or the joyful looks their parents give them after the game, makes it worthwhile. Without people volunteering, Mountview Boys and Girls FC would be no more. That's why I do it, and that's why I value volunteering so much.

(91 words)

As explained in the earlier lesson, this is a very personal paragraph from the **article writer's** point of view. Now, let's look at a sample that includes **investigation**.

I wanted to find out the value that volunteering has for my local community, so I went down to my local Men's Shed charity. I'd heard about it, but I had no idea what it was about. The leader is a guy called Mike. He is from New Zealand but has lived in Ireland for years. I asked him what the sheds are all about. 'It is an organisation that encourages men, especially older ones, to get together on a weekly basis to build things and chat,' Mike replied.

The logo for the Irish Men's Shed Association. What do you think of the symbols of the open door and the hands shaking?

'But why is it needed?' was my next question.

'Well,' continued Mike, after a little bit of thought. 'There are loads of clubs for kids and teenagers, but not much for older blokes. That can make them feel a bit isolated and alone. We were set up to show them that you can still have the craic, learn new skills and pass on some of your own, no matter what age you are.' There was a certain pride in Mike's voice as he said this, and the value of Men's Sheds really hit me then.

(184 words over 3 paragraphs)

1. How do we see **investigation** in the opening two sentences? _____

   _____

   _____

2. What do we learn about Men's Sheds in the first paragraph? _____

   _____

   _____

3. How does Mike explain the value of Men's Sheds in the last paragraph? _____

   _____

   _____

4. How do we know Mike's words had an **impact** on the writer? _____

   _____

   _____

Question analysis

The question below should also look very familiar. You will have planned and answered this in **Lesson 10** as well. But that was only for 50 marks. Now you need to do more **planning** because the examiner expects twice as much content from you.

Question – 100 marks

Write an article, to be published in a popular magazine, on the value of volunteering with at least one sporting or charitable organisation. The article should discuss the possible benefits for the people who volunteer their time and energy, and for the organisation(s) involved.

> The (s) at the end of organisation means that the 's' is optional. So you could just talk about one organisation if you want, or many organisations. The (s) just gives you a choice.

---

1. What magazine are you going to write for? _____

2. In your own words, what does the 'value of volunteering' mean? _____
   _____

3. What organisations are you allowed to talk about volunteering in? _____
   _____

4. Are you only allowed to talk about one organisation? _____

5. Reread the last line and number the things you are being asked to talk about in your article.

The **structure** of an **article** is the same as the one in **Lesson 10** (page 50). The only real difference is what is needed in the **main body** paragraphs.

Structure – Article

The main body of the answer

- **Ten to 12** planned **IRE** paragraphs of about 70 to 80 words each are needed for a 100-mark composition.

- Each **idea** can be explored over **two to three paragraphs**.

- You will need paragraphs that include:

  - Personal reflection on the topic

  - Investigation of the subject

  - Conversations with people involved (see **Lesson 14** (page 67) for information on writing conversations)

The main body of the answer

These sections of two to three paragraphs need **planning**.

The first part of the **plan** is to write down the **idea** you will talk about.

The second part is to say how you will **investigate** it. Who could you talk to? Where could you look for **information**? What did you find out? Was your opinion changed? Was your original view confirmed?

Now you can fully **plan** the 100-mark **composition** question:

What are the benefits for the people who volunteer their time and energy?

1. It makes them feel better knowing that they are supporting their community.

    • I could talk to the leader of the local Men's Shed.

2. It gives them a chance to make new friends.

    • I could speak with the coaches of the local football teams and ask them if they are mates with the other coaches.

3. _____

    • _____

4. _____

    • _____

5. _____

    • _____

What benefits are there for the organisations?

1. They would not be able to run without people donating their time.

    • I could ask the local football coach what would happen if _____

2. It spreads the name of the organisation in the community.

    • I could check the local newspaper for _____

3. _____

    • _____

4. _____

    • _____

This is a word cloud on volunteering. Choose five of the most important words in it and say why they stand out to you.

Time to Write

If you want to work on an **introduction**, go back to **Lesson 10** for what to include. In this lesson, we are going to only work on the **investigation** paragraphs. Look at the sample paragraph below. It explains the **idea** that charities need volunteers or else they will not be able to function.

> So, could charitable organisations actually run without the help of volunteers? From my experience, no. These organisations, like the local Foróige club for teens in my area, rely on volunteers because, without them, there simply isn't the funding to keep the charity going. Where will the government find millions of euro to pay the people who are already doing the work out of love and community pride? The money value of volunteering can be seen quite well here because without people providing their time and energy for nothing, the clubs wouldn't run.
>
> (92 words)

For the **100-mark composition**, you will need to go into more detail and **investigate** the **idea**. Next, practise an interview style with the person who runs the club:

Make up a name and job title for the person you're talking to. → To find out more, I caught up with _____

_____

What did you ask them about volunteering at the club? Use direct speech. → I asked them, _____

_____

_____

What did they say back? Again, use direct speech. → Their response really made me think. They said, _____

_____

Refer to the question and use the key question words. → Their words really showed me _____

_____

_____

 # Time to Finish

With your answer planned and some sample paragraphs done, it's now time to complete your answer on a separate page.

*Some methods of research are mentioned in the **Time to Impress** examples. Can you think of any more?*

 **Time to Impress**

Do some digging

A key aspect of being an **investigator** is digging into things that other people may have overlooked. This shows your skill and dedication as a **journalist**, and really adds a sense of realness to your **article**. Finish the samples below.

1. Once I'd heard about the local GAA club, I decided to do some digging. It was founded in 1917 by Michael O'Hare, and twelve All-Ireland winners have come through its ranks.

2. Once the police released the name, I decided to investigate some more. What I found out about them was _____
   _____

3. So what makes the perfect music festival? My online research has shown me _____
   _____
   _____

4. I looked into the latest opinion polls about our local politicians and found _____
   _____
   _____

Class/Homework exercise

- Read and analyse the following questions.
- Then plan out your answers.
- Finally, write a full 100-mark answer.

1. Write an article for a magazine popular with young people, in which you outline what you think you, and young people generally, could do to help build better lives for people in your community, and in the world generally. (2018)

2. You have been asked to write an article for a magazine popular with young people. In your article you should give advice to Leaving Certificate students on how to develop their study skills, maintain a healthy lifestyle while preparing for exams, and balance study with more social aspects of life. (2017)

3. Write an article for a travel magazine, in which you encourage young people to visit Ireland, telling them why they should come here, and what you recommend they should see and do during their visit. (2016)

 Time to Reflect

1. How is an **article** different to a **news report**?
2. What is the biggest planning difference between a 50-mark and a 100-mark question?
3. What **tone** should an article be written in?
4. How important is **investigation** in an **article**?
5. Should you include personal experience in an **article**? Why?
6. What do interviews add to **articles**?